Vera Peiffer is a qualifie~~~ ~~~ighly successful priva~~~ ~~~ps for Positive Think~~~ ~~~ngland and Germany and~~~ ~~~ation, an organization w~~~ ~~~ teaching practical life skills.

If you would like more information on seminars or the Positive Thinking Correspondence Course, you can contact Vera at:

The Peiffer Foundation
P.O. Box 2517
London W5 5LN

POSITIVELY FEARLESS

BREAKING FREE OF THE FEARS
THAT HOLD YOU BACK

Vera Peiffer

ELEMENT
Shaftesbury, Dorset • Boston, Massachusetts
Melbourne, Victoria

...ited 1999
...r 1993

...K in 1993 by
Element Books Limited

This edition published in the UK in 1999 by
Element Books Limited
Shaftesbury, Dorset SP7 8BP

Published in the USA in 1999 by
Element Books, Inc.
160 North Washington Street
Boston, MA 02114

Published in Australia in 1999 by
Element Books and distributed
by Penguin Australia Limited
487 Maroondah Highway, Ringwood
Victoria 3134

Vera Peiffer has asserted her right under the
Copyright, Designs and Patents Act, 1988
to be identified as the author of this work.

Cover design by Slatter-Anderson
Design by Roger Lightfoot
Typeset by Poole Typesetting, Bournemouth, Dorset
Printed and bound in Great Britain by
J. W. Arrowsmith Ltd, Bristol

British Libary Cataloguing in Publication
data available

Library of Congress Cataloging in Publication
data available

ISBN 1 86204 6220

Contents

To dear Pia Slongo,
with love and gratitude
for making my childhood
bearable.

To the man who is afraid,
everything rustles.

Sophocles, Fragment 58, Acrisius

Introduction

He unlocked the heavy oak door that led down to the cellars of the university and motioned the others to follow him. He shone his torch in front of him, illuminating the narrow, steep steps that led down into the maze of vaults that lay underneath the main building.

There were five of them filing down the old stone steps: four members of the fraternity, recognizable by the caps and bands they were wearing, and one applicant, a dark haired, rather pale young man called Richard who wished to join the fraternity.

He had not been told where they were going to take him, and he knew, without anyone telling him, that it would have been bad form to ask. It would have been like admitting that he was worried, which of course he was; so he just followed the student in front of him. Nobody was speaking.

Richard was second in line, with three students following behind him. He felt very nearly like a prisoner, even though he knew nobody was forcing him to do this. It was not so much the students behind him that forced him but his own pride that compelled him to go on. If he backed out now, he would lose face, he would be regarded as a coward and be the laughing stock of the college. Therefore he decided that it was now simply a matter of pulling himself together and going through with it.

They reached the bottom of the steps which led them into a musty smelling vault where tools and various materials that were needed for the maintenance of the college were kept. It was chilly down here, and Richard felt the cold from the bare stone floor creeping through the soles of his shoes up into his legs. He noticed with some alarm that it was already impossible to hear any sounds or voices from upstairs; only their own steps echoed hollowly in the windowless basement room as they crossed over to another door.

The student with the torch produced a second key and ceremoniously unlocked the door. Before he opened it, he turned around to Richard and shone the torch in his direction. 'Your task,' he said in a low, matter-of-fact voice, 'is to stay in the room beyond this door for the next hour. Once you have entered the room, I will lock the door behind you. In an hour, we will be back to let you out.' One of the other students gave a brief laugh and added ominously, 'Unless we forget . . . !' Richard felt a lump in his throat and his heart beating faster.

The student with the torch opened the door just enough for Richard to squeeze through into the room beyond, holding the light well away from the door so that Richard was unable to see the interior. As soon as Richard had entered the room, the door behind him slammed shut, and a moment later he heard the key turn in the lock. He heard a muffled, 'Have fun!', then retreating steps, then nothing.

And then there was only silence and darkness. Utter darkness. Richard stood very still. The only thing he could hear was his breathing. He kept his back firmly pressed against the door, waiting, hoping that his eyes would adapt to the darkness in a little while so that he could see where he was. He did not know how big the room was, or what shape it was or what was in it. He stared longingly into the darkness and waited, waited, his eyes forced wide open. He turned his head slowly from right to left, hoping to detect an outline of something, but he could not see. For a moment he felt as if he had gone blind, and he could feel a sudden panic rising in him. He started to shiver, his heart thundered in his chest and he noticed suddenly that his hands had become clammy.

With his back firmly pressed against the door, he slid slowly down into a sitting position until he felt the stone floor under his backside. He cowered for a while, listening to the darkness. The air was stale and cool against his face. He strained his ears for sounds around him, sitting quite still. His rapid breathing frightened him. What if there were mice here or, even worse, rats? The college grounds were infested with them, everyone knew that. He started shaking again. He was hugging his knees for warmth and he knew that the knuckles of his fingers were white with tension. The cold from the floor was beginning to creep into his bones and he realized that he would not be able to remain seated for long.

He tried to put the thought of rats out of his mind, but without success. His fear was beginning to become a thing in itself which he could not control any longer. Anxious thoughts made his head spin. Not being able to see his surroundings made him feel helpless and exposed and he became aware of cold sweat breaking out on his forehead. He decided to stand up again to get most of his body away from the ground which was where the rats would be if there were any. He slid up slowly, his back pressed against the door, still shaking, still listening and staring at the invisible floor. How long had he been in here now? He didn't have his watch on him; they had made him leave it behind in his room when they came to collect him. But he could not have seen what the time was in this pitch darkness anyway . . .

He forced himself to think rationally. He would only be in here for an hour, in fact less than an hour because some time had already elapsed since he entered the room. He would just stand here by the door and count the minutes as they ticked by until his time was up and they came to get him. If they didn't forget him, that was. If they did, he could die down here. Even if he screamed, nobody would hear him. Maybe there was a skeleton somewhere in this room, the remains of someone who had been forgotten down here. This sudden thought was so powerful that he decided not to move from his present position so as not to touch anything, dead or alive, that might be in the room.

He felt he had been standing there for an eternity, his feet and legs tired but tensely pressed together, his arms hugging his shoulders. He just could not stop thinking about the rats when suddenly his heart nearly stopped — there had been a sound from the left. Or at least he *thought* there was a sound. He held his breath in case the sound reoccurred, at the same time slowly turning his head in the direction from where the little whispering noise seemed to have emanated.

All his senses were on alert, he could feel every muscle and every fibre of his body getting rigid and his breath coming in quick, shallow puffs as if he had been running. He was petrified with fear. What if that rat was creeping up on him slowly? They were very clever animals, everyone knew that. They could probably see in the dark. His mind was suddenly flooded with all those stories he had read or heard of rats attacking people, running up people's legs and biting them in the face or going for their throat with those razorsharp teeth . . . He could only just stifle a scream.

Suddenly, *there*! Another sound, this time from further over to the right! The rat was moving about, or even worse, there were *several* of them. Richard was panting. They lived in colonies, didn't they? His scalp was creeping and he felt his whole body covered in goosebumps.

Even though he could not see anything, he didn't dare close his eyes. He was straining to hear any further sounds so he would know how fast they were advancing. His back hurt with the pressure against the door but he could not ease it; the door was his only point of reference in the room and he preferred to endure the piercing pain that was running along his bony spine, rather than let go of his landmark. Sweat began to trickle down his face, running down into his collar. They were approaching him rapidly now; they were fast animals and they were vicious if you invaded their territory. *There*! Something had brushed past his trouserleg, he had felt it quite distinctly. Automatically he kicked his leg forward as if to shake off an attacker, thinking simultaneously, 'This will only make them more hostile,' but he could not stop himself any more: his leg was kicking, kicking, in a frenzy, out of control, as if it was no longer part of his body but a thing in itself, just frantically kicking at his invisible attackers.

He pressed into the door behind him, sobbing, when suddenly the door gave and he fell backwards out of the room into bright lights. He had not heard them coming back and unlocking the door. He covered his eyes with his hand against the sudden brightness of the light and also because he didn't want them to see that he had been crying. He breathed deeply, trying to collect himself, and finally took his hand away. As he looked up he noticed that all the students were carrying torches now. He rubbed his eyes and scrambled to his feet, brushing down his clothes to cover up his embarrassment.

And now, something peculiar happened. One by one, the students went past him into the room where he had spent the last horrible hour, illuminating the room with their torches.

Richard could now see that the room was small, without windows, with a stone floor, stone walls and a stone ceiling. And he could see another thing – the room was TOTALLY EMPTY.

Anyone who has suffered from a phobia will have recognized in this story the physical and emotional sensations that assail you when you encounter (or even only think about) the feared object or situation. As soon as the mind registers the first 'danger' signals, it switches into overdrive – your heart races, you start sweating, you get hot and cold and feel you are frozen to the spot for one awful second, and then you panic, and the only thing you can do at that moment is to run away as fast as you can.

We can all sympathize with this reaction when a person finds themselves face to face with a growling Rottweiler. In this context, we find the fear understandable and therefore 'normal'. However, with phobias the fear-inducing object or situation is one that is commonly regarded as innocuous. People with phobias can be terrorstricken when faced with a sparrow on the pavement or when they are asked to enter a lift. Now, their fear doesn't make any sense to us because it strikes us as irrational.

Longman's Dictionary of Psychology and Psychiatry defines fear as follows:

> FEAR an intense emotion aroused by a recognized threat, and involving a feeling of unpleasant tension, a strong impulse to escape, and physiological reactions, such as rapid heartbeat, tensing of the muscles, and in general, mobilization of the organism for flight or fight. F. is aroused not only by direct danger but by situations and objects that represent this danger. See PHOBIA. Also see ANXIETY.

Fear, in one form or another, is very much an everyday occurrence in our lives. When we worry about that meeting we have to attend in the afternoon, we are fearful of what might happen. When we feel apprehensive as we prepare food for a dinner party in the evening, we experience a mild form of fear. Whatever the level, fear always entails an expectation of things going wrong; in other words, fear is projected disaster-thinking.

Fear is a very powerful restrictive force which can have a fundamental influence on our lives. It stops us from doing what we want to do, it forces us to do things we don't want to do, it hinders our progress and prevents us from developing to our full potential.

Fear pervades all our lives to a certain extent, its manifestations ranging from mild apprehension to fully fledged phobias and anxiety attacks. Often, we are at a loss what to do about it because it can seem to be irrational and therefore unmanageable. To many people, their fear feels like something within themselves but outside their control.

This book deals with the positive and negative aspects of fear and explains how fear comes about. You will also find out about the connections between the physical and mental symptoms of fear, how they are first established and how this can then become a self-perpetuating problem. Whether an individual reacts with fear to any given situation is dependent on many factors, such as the person's present frame of mind or state of health, their individual likes and dislikes. Other contributory factors can be stress within the family or at work.

Any object or situation can lead to anxiety, and the more absurd the object of the fear, the more difficult it seems to be to resolve the problem.

This book explores the underlying principles that govern the occurrence of fear, but over and above these theoretical explanations you will find described a range of methods as used in modern psychotherapy and self-help programmes which enable the individual to deal with and overcome fears. In cases where the fear is only slight, it can be combated with methods like relaxation, gradual desensitization or visualization. Nearly all the methods introduced in the book are suitable as self-help programmes which you can apply at home. When used regularly over a period of several weeks, these techniques have proved to be highly successful. In cases where the fear appears to be irrational or too severe to handle without outside help, an analytical approach carried out by a therapist can help resolve the fear problem.

The essential message of the book is that there is no need to live with fear you don't want. Just because you cannot see a solution does not mean there isn't one. *Positively Fearless* shows ways out of fear which enable you to lead a richer and freer life and have the confidence to fulfil your potential. Others have done it, and if only *one* other person in the world can do it, so can you!

PART ONE

The Nature of Fear

1. Causes and Effects

In this chapter, we will be looking at the various ways in which fears can develop and how, once they are fully-fledged, they can affect us.

Some fears occur as an inevitable by-product of growing up and often disappear when we are older; other fears are generated by traumatic incidents or are inflicted through exposure to an unfavourable social environment. Another factor that can result in experiencing fear is change. Change always creates a certain amount of emotional upheaval, whether the change is positive or negative. A promotion at work can be just as stressful as a car accident!

Once a fear has registered in our mind for the first time, it becomes part of our emotional experience. If we imagine our memory as being a lump of malleable substance, then any experience we have leaves a trace in that substance, like a groove. If an event is coupled with a strong emotion, such as fear, the trace will cut more deeply into the substance, and the more often a fear-inducing event takes place, the deeper the groove will become so that the mind will latch into that groove ever more readily on subsequent occasions. The effect is that we begin to respond automatically with fear when that event occurs; in other words, we go onto 'auto-pilot'.

The effect fear has on body and mind is quite substantial. It brings about changes in the body which are noticeable even to a layperson. We can observe someone tensing up, going white as a sheet or 'freezing' as they get frightened. But even more important than those outward reactions is what happens inside the body: measurable chemical changes take place which, in severe cases, can upset the physical equilibrium to an extent where you can develop a physical illness if you experience this fear on a regular basis.

But first, let us look at fear in general terms, its original advantages and how these advantages can become detrimental.

POSITIVE AND NEGATIVE FEAR

Fear is an emotional response that acts as a warning signal when we are in a situation that we perceive as being dangerous. This is fine as long as the situation *is* indeed hazardous and threatens our life or physical well-being. It is useful and indeed life-saving when you stay away from the edge of a cliff while a strong wind is blowing; it is commendable to stay clear of a big dog that growls at you; it makes sense to start running when your house is on fire. In all of these cases, fear acts as a positive, protective impulse that mobilizes you for flight so that you can remove yourself from the dangerous situation.

This in-built mechanism works from a very young age. This was shown in experiments where babies who had just learnt to crawl were left to move about freely on a surface that looked as if it was dropping off steeply in the middle. Even though the 'abyss' was covered by a strong sheet of glass, none of the babies would attempt to crawl past the edge. Equally, most children have a healthy respect for animals that are as large or larger than they are and will not approach them unless encouraged by an adult who needs to demonstrate repeatedly that the animal is harmless.

Fear is positive when it prevents us from coming to harm on a physical level, but nowadays there are not that many situations in everyday life where our life is in jeopardy. Whereas a few thousand years ago, man was physically threatened by wild animals, tempestuous weather and other outside hazards, we now have a comparatively easy life where the basic necessities are provided for. The wildest animal most of us will ever come in contact with is the neighbour's cat; solid houses protect us against bad weather and modern medicine and healthcare prolong our life to a multiple of what the Neanderthal man could hope to reach — and yet, fear is still around.

It seems as if modern times impose a different sort of fear on us, a fear that wants to protect us from *emotional* threats such as feelings of being worthless or unloved or unwanted. While you are physically unsafe there is not a lot of time to worry about these things – the lowest suicide rate is always during times of war. It is when we can feel secure in our basic physical needs that we seem to permit ourselves to fret over other, less dire situations. In fact, when we look at the fears we experience today, we can see that these are mainly concerned with things that *might happen* to us, rather than with things that *are actually happening* at the moment. We occupy our minds with imagined future calamities, such as 'What if I go overdrawn?' and 'What if I am asked to speak at the conference tomorrow?' and 'What if the man I fancy rejects me?' These negative mental projections are commonly known as 'worries', and they often make us miss out on the here and now because we are too busy worrying about tomorrow.

It is at this point that fear can potentially lose its positive aspect and turn into a negative force. As long as you use your fear as a warning signal and take action to sort out your difficulties, the fear retains its positive function. If you are worried about your financial situation and, as a consequence, make an appointment with your bank manager to talk things through, then this is a constructive way of dealing with the fear and will ultimately result in solving the problem that originally caused the fear. If, however, you allow things to get out of hand by acting passively and by avoiding looking at the problem, the fear can get out of proportion. In the case of financial problems, a passive 'worrier' may for example decide not to look at statements or letters from the bank any more, hoping that the whole problem will somehow go away by itself.

Some people are able to use their fear creatively to achieve their aims. They use their anxiety as an impetus to propel them forward to achieve new and better things, to help them focus their mind and heighten their awareness for new opportunities; in other words, the fear acts as a motivating force. This way, the extra energy that is created by anxiety is channelled in a positive way and ultimately dispels the fear.

Passive worriers, on the other hand, are refusing to deal with their problem, they just sit back and suffer, frightened of what might happen, and it is this type of fear that is very negative indeed. As it is not cut short by action, it will persist in the person's mind until they finally start sorting out their problem.

If you procrastinate and draw out the time during which you remain passive, you expose yourself to an inordinate measure of fear and worry, and this has a number of detrimental side-effects.

As we shall see in a later chapter, the experience of fear affects us on a physical level. Adrenalin is pumped out and blood sugars are released into the blood stream, all of which help hype up the body for action. This is still the ancient caveman-response where extra energy was needed to either run away as fast as possible or fight as fiercely as possible in order to survive. Today, these are hardly appropriate responses, and so more often than not, we are unable to make use of that extra energy that has been automatically provided by the body. This means that the energy is racing around inside the body, producing a racing heart beat, racing thoughts and consequently feelings of physical and mental discomfort, also known as stress.

When a person experiences stressful situations on a regular basis and is unable or unwilling to resolve them, the body is exposed to an overload of adrenalin and, as a consequence, becomes chemically unbalanced. This link between illness and emotional stress has been substantiated by studies in America. Janice and Ronald Kiecolt Glaser at Ohio University did some pioneer research into psycho-neuro-immunology, a new term for the study of how psychological factors affect the immune system. During stressful periods the body produces large amounts of a steroid called cortisol. This inhibits the work of macrophage cells which are a key part of our immune system – they digest the debris of dead cells in the bloodstream and they summon other defences such as T-cells when they encounter a virus, bacterium or other foreign organism. If their action is inhibited, this means the body can no longer respond normally to infection. The immune system is weakened and you are much more likely to catch an illness that is going around, such as the flu or a stomach bug, than when you are on an emotionally even keel.

Another aspect that can make fear into a negative force is that it can upset your emotional balance to an extent where you cannot function properly any more. You are confused, agitated without release, and you find it difficult to make decisions. You may feel tearful or aggressive and feel out of control. In severe cases, this can lead to a nervous breakdown.

When you are afraid too often or for too long, fear becomes very negative indeed and needs to be dealt with. The more actively and openly you address problems in your life, the less fear you will experience when other problems come along. The more experienced you are in solving problems, the less frightening they become. There are always ways out of problems, even if the problem is a fear, for example if you suffer from a phobia. There will be more on how to resolve fears in Chapter 3 of this book.

Initial Occurrence and Self-Perpetuation

Sigmund Freud stated that there are certain phenomena, such as snakes, that arouse anxiety in most humans, and he therefore called these fears *universal phobias*. He offset these universal phobias against *specific phobias* which involve those things that do not normally produce fear, for example cats.

Let us assume that Freud was right and that there are certain fears that are instinctive and present from the moment we are born, and that there are other fears that we acquire at some later point in our life. This would mean that some fears are natural because they are inborn, whereas others are anomalous because they are not part of our biological make-up. This could well be a reason why so many people don't seek help for an irrational fear they experience, simply because they feel silly for being afraid of something that no one else is afraid of.

People tend to hesitate quite a long time before they get professional assistance with their particular fear. This is because when a fear occurs for the first time, it often takes place in a very logical context. Your partner criticizes you a lot and you become afraid of trying out new things. Someone drives their car into the back of yours and you have a shock. A dog jumps up at you and barks fiercely and you are terrified. Your parents are overdemanding and you become a perfectionist who is afraid of failure.

All these situations will produce a certain degree of discomfort and fear in you as they occur for the first time. Incidents like the car accident and the fierce dog are usually one-off occasions, whereas the critical partner or the overdemanding parent scenarios are ongoing – as long as you are with these people, you are exposed to their influence and thereby to the anxiety-inducing atmosphere. This is of course significant when we are looking at whether the fear will persist once the original event has passed. With sudden, one-off shocks like the accident or the dog, it will depend on the frame of mind you are in and on the accompanying circumstances. If your life and your emotions have been reasonably balanced before the shock occurs, chances are that you will feel fearful about similar situations for a while to come, but with time, the fear dwindles until it has gone down to a normal level. At this point, you may still feel slightly cautious when you see a dog or you may check your rear view mirror more than you used to in the past, but you no longer experience the physical symptoms of fear. Once a fear is reduced to this level, we can accept it quite easily because we can now describe it as 'common sense caution' which we can accept as a normal result of a learning experience.

Things look different, however, when we are already feeling low at the time when the shock occurs. We are now much more vulnerable and therefore more likely to experience the event as traumatic. It will take us much longer to get over the shock and we are more likely to develop a phobic reaction as a consequence. This could mean that we now begin to avoid driving the car or we now shun all dogs. Initially we do so to help ourselves recover from the shock, but often this avoidance strategy becomes a habit. Because we have not exposed ourselves to the situation for a while, we become more and more afraid of it. This is why riding instructors will always ask you to get back into the saddle when you have fallen off; that way there is no time for you to establish an avoidance pattern.

When your fear started because of the way another person reacts or behaves towards you, matters become more complicated, especially when you spend a lot of time with that person, for example if you live with them. When someone is overcritical of you and you are exposed to their disapproval on a daily basis, then this has a brain-washing effect – you get used to it.

Before you get used to it, you normally go through a period of being upset about the constant criticism, but since you cannot live with being upset all the time, you resign yourself to it and eventually end up believing what is said about you, at least on a subconsious level. Consciously you may fight the accusation, but subconsciously a little doubt starts creeping in. 'No smoke without fire!' you think to yourself, and the next time you catch yourself making a mistake you shudder: the other person was right after all! Your self-confidence sinks yet a bit lower, and next time you are faced with an unusual task, you ask someone else to do it . . . As a consequence, you get less practice trying out new things, you become less competent and therefore more afraid and you start regarding yourself as useless. At this point, you have usually lost sight of what started this downhill process in the first place. All that is left is your fear, clearly visible to you and everyone around you.

HOW FEAR COMES ABOUT

When a child is born, it brings with it a set of characteristics which manifest themselves in the child's personality. From the very start, there are children who are bolder and less fearful than others. You only need to look at a family with several children. Any mother will tell you how different her children were right from the start. One is extrovert and always up to something, the other one is shy and won't easily approach unknown situations or people.

However, these genetically determined personality traits can undergo changes, depending on the responses that the child gets to different patterns of behaviour. If outgoing behaviour is labelled 'naughty' by an anxious parent, a lively child will learn to become cautious and suppress its curiosity. Or alternatively, it will continue to do the same things, but secretly, thereby imbuing the erstwhile pleasurable activity with guilt.

If a child is shy to start with and the mother prevents the child's attempts to explore the world with nervous remonstrations, the child will eventually give up trying and end up less skilful in tackling unknown situations because he or she has not practised doing so. On the other hand, if a shy child is gently encouraged and praised for any progress, he has every chance of overcoming his fears.

Children spend their early years trying to make sense of the world around them. As we have seen in Richard's story in the introduction to the book, the unknown can easily evoke anxiety in us. Put yourself into a child's shoes for a moment. How strange everything must seem from the perspective of a three-year-old who gazes at his chair in the corner of the room which looks like a monster at night when the lights are out and the bedroom is dim. Try and remember again for a moment what it feels like to be totally and utterly dependent on your parents for love, comfort, approval, food, warmth and a roof over your head. You feel helpless and vulnerable because there are millions of things out there that you cannot make head or tail of. So in order to understand these matters, you find your own explanations, based on your knowledge of the world which consists of fairy tales, picture books, television, nursery school and the way your parents treat you and one another.

Since you are new to the job as member of the human race you get things wrong a lot, and there is usually someone there to point it out to you. Life is confusing and everything is new, your body, your feelings, your struggles with learning. From the moment you are born you are launched into the great unknown. It is not really surprising that you are sometimes afraid, is it?

Childhood fears

Children copy what they see and hear. They not only copy words and phrases, they also copy gestures, behaviour and the feelings that go with the behaviour. Watch a mother pointing at a spider with a disgusted face in the presence of a child!

Copying fears is not confined to the childhood period; it can also happen later on in life, but the possibility of 'catching' a fear off someone else is generally more likely during the formative years. If you spend your childhood in an environment where anger is taboo and where differences are never discussed openly, you learn to fear arguments. The fact that a certain issue is avoided in a family makes that very issue all the more mysterious and therefore more alarming. As long as a fear remains in your head without being openly admitted and talked about, the fear can become a thing in itself and grow out of proportion, especially with children who have a much more vivid imagination than adults.

Adults often assume that children lead a privileged existence because they don't have to worry about money or work. Children don't have the responsibilities adults have and therefore, it is concluded erroneously, they have nothing to worry about. But children suffer from fear just as adults do, only children experience fears as more overwhelming and they don't always have the ability to express those fears in words. When there are sudden crashing sounds outside you may feel like the world is coming to an end and you are petrified – because you don't know that this is a natural phenomenon called a thunderstorm. When that big animal appears before you, your heart nearly stops – because you don't know that this is the neighbours' dog who is perfectly friendly and harmless.

Some parents feel that they should not pamper their child too much, and they therefore ignore it when the child is afraid at night and cries. They assume that by letting the child deal with the fear by itself they prevent the child from getting spoilt, when quite the opposite is true. A child that is left to its own fears will feel abandoned and extremely helpless and will therefore be less able to cope with fear situations later on in life. A child that receives no positive help and support as it is trying to come to terms with the world around it doesn't become tougher but, on the contrary, weaker. It is by leaving your child to cry that you spoil it, and it is by punishing your child for feeling afraid that you spoil your child's chances of becoming a confident person.

Children are sometimes discouraged from learning to cope with fears by the negative responses they get when they are afraid. When a child is being punished for being afraid, it will end up trying to avoid the frightening situation. This is most likely to occur when the parents themselves are unable to admit to their own fears; instead of saying that they are worried about something, they shout or are in a bad mood or withdraw. The child is then left with the shameful, albeit erroneous, impression that he or she is the only one who experiences fear. And as children always blame themselves for anything that goes wrong, they tend to link up their fear with a sense of guilt of being inadequate, so they end up not only being handicapped by the fear itself, but also by the connotations of failure that this fear has for them.

The fiercer the parents' rejection of the child's fears, the fiercer the child's inner self-accusations will be − and the more likely it is that the child will copy the parents' vehement responses in later life.

Fear through exhaustion

Having looked at how fears can develop in childhood, let us now turn to problematic situations later on in life. In some instances, you may well be surprised at the factors that can lead to the experience of fear − we often underestimate the influence everyday events can have on us.

If you are under constant or prolonged pressure at work, you can become stressed, and this in turn leads to fatigue and weariness. When your body and mind are exposed to physical overload, you will come to the point where you begin to weaken physically. This state of exhaustion can be evoked by exaggerated physical activity, such as exercising vigorously when you are ill, or lifting and carrying heavy items. The solution here is obvious − you get some sleep, take it easy the next day and allow your body to regain strength.

Physically exhausting activities are usually not a problem, especially when they are linked to a feeling of enjoyment or a sense of achievement. A problem arises only when these activities become an unpleasant chore or if you overdo it and have to push yourself to perform them. If, for example, you are a mother with several children, one of whom is handicapped, you will not only have to do all the washing, shopping and cleaning and looking after the healthy children, you will also have to attend to the special needs of your handicapped child which means that you are juggling a hundred things and work your body very hard. Unless you get a break every once in a while, you will have a problem with physical exhaustion. As a consequence, you feel overwhelmed by all your tasks because you

have become physically unable to accomplish them satisfactorily; life is getting on top of you, you feel you cannot cope any
more. It is in a situation like this that people can (but don't
necessarily have to) develop seemingly irrational fears like
agoraphobia.

The same mechanics apply to situations where there is an
overload of mental activity. Even though you are sitting behind
a desk without physically exerting yourself, extreme or prolonged pressures on your ability to make decisions and cope
with difficult or unpleasant situations have the same effect on
your body as running a marathon. Whether you are a secretary
or a foreman or the manager of your department, the moment
you have more to do than you feel you can handle, you will
become tired.

What makes matters worse is that it is often exceedingly
difficult to get the rest you need, simply because you can't just
walk away from your job. Therefore you keep on pushing
yourself harder and harder and putting further pressure on a
body that is already exhausted. Because you are tired, you feel
less able to cope with your work, and therefore you feel more
anxious. Because you feel more anxious, you are more likely to
make mistakes which in turn confirms your doubts about your
ability to cope. This process can easily spiral further down so
that a person feels constantly anxious and becomes afraid of
situations they could handle quite easily beforehand when they
were refreshed and physically strong.

A client of mine told me once that she knows exactly at what
point she is overworked. As she is going to sleep at night she
suddenly seems to notice a little animal running across her bed,
and this jerks her awake with momentary terror. (It is interesting to note in this context that this client does not have any
phobias concerning small animals when she is awake.)

When she switches on the light she invariably finds that
there is no animal, but she now finds it difficult to go back to
sleep because her whole body is tensed up with the shock.

Her recipe to get rid of these hallucinations is to have a very
quiet time when she gets home from work. As she cannot cut
down on the amount of work she needs to do she tackles the
problem by relaxing in the evenings, which means no television, no radio, and instead reading or doing a jigsaw puzzle or

taking a hot bath. That way she is keeping stimulation to a minimum, and after two or three days, her sleeping pattern returns to normal.

Fear through stressful change

As we go through everyday life we establish certain routines and ways in which we deal with things. There is a certain order in which we organize our movements in the morning before we leave for the office. We go into the bathroom first, then we put the kettle on while we are getting dressed, then we make the tea or coffee and butter the toast while we have a quick look at the newspaper, and then we leave the house.

If we have a partner, we will have negotiated in the beginning who is to use the bathroom first, so our habitual pattern is rearranged in a manner which hopefully is agreeable to both parties. You acknowledge the fact that your wife likes to have the toothpaste squeezed from the bottom and the cap put back on, so you do this; your wife knows that you hate to use soap with hairs stuck to it, so she makes sure the soap is clean after she has used it. So far so good.

Now a friend of yours comes to stay for a while. His girlfriend has thrown him out and has changed the locks on the door so he cannot get into his own flat. You invite him to stay with you until he has found somewhere else. You know he has already looked at a flat to rent and it is likely that he will only be staying with you for a week. Nevertheless, a change occurs in your daily routine since there are now three people sharing the house instead of two. You agree on a new rota for using the bathroom in the mornings, and it all works very well, except for the fact that your friend squeezes your toothpaste in the middle (he forgot to get his own) and leaves hair on the soap. He also takes a long time to get out of the shower which makes you more pushed for time, but you don't say too much because it is only for a week. And anyway, your friend is very helpful; he does the washing-up after dinner, although he doesn't rinse the cutlery with clear water after he has washed it as you would prefer him to do. He also sits in your chair when you all arrive home from work, and you cannot watch your favourite television programme because you want to give him time to discuss his present problems.

You really like your friend who is a kind and polite person, and you don't for a minute begrudge the hospitality you have extended. It makes you feel good that you are able to help and you are pleased when he tells you at the end of the week how grateful he is for your support – and yet, you feel a sense of relief when he has finally gone because now you have more time in the bathroom again, the toothpaste gets squeezed in the right place, the soap will be clean and you can sit in your chair and watch your favourite programme, secure in the knowledge that the cutlery has been rinsed in clear water before it went back into the drawer.

You may laugh and find this account of events exaggerated, but think about it! If you are honest with yourself, you have to admit that you, too, have certain routines in your life which you don't like to see interrupted and certain ways of doing things which you tend to adhere to. This goes both for your private life and your life outside the home.

We all have established patterns at work which we strive to maintain if at all possible. We look at the in-tray first and then take off our coat. Or we have a cup of coffee first and then look at the mail.

The routines we create for ourselves have the purpose of making us feel as comfortable as possible. We usually devise routines that are the most favourable, convenient and pleasant way of doing things. The reason why we want to sit in a particular armchair in the evenings is that this chair is closest to the drinks cabinet or because it is softer than the sofa or because the view on to the street is better. The reason why we leave the filing to the last moment is because we don't like doing it, so we do other things first which don't make us feel uncomfortable. The reason why we look at the in-tray first is that we find it re-assuring to know straight away what needs to be done during the working day. If you are a different personality type you will have a cup of tea first because you feel more comfortable easing yourself into work gently and acclimatizing to the thought that you will eventually have to do some work for the money they pay you . . .

The routines that we establish for ourselves are very individual and tailor-made as closely as possible to our needs; they reflect our priorities in life.

As we have seen in the above example of the friend who came to stay for a week, even a comparatively minor deviation from your daily routine has a certain stressful effect. Depending on the individuals involved, this stress will be felt more or less strongly. At the level described in the above examples, it is unlikely that anxiety or fear will arise since the overall stress level is too low. Both the host and the friend who comes to stay like one another; the host's wife readily agrees to take the friend in, and the period of time where the daily routine needs to be altered is limited to a tolerable length.

But consider a slightly different scenario. The person who comes to stay is the first baby of a married couple. Up to now, they have enjoyed long lie-ins on weekends, a busy social life, having friends round, going to the cinema and theatre. They make spontaneous decisions when they want to go on holiday, packing and going whenever they please, often on the spur of the moment.

All this comes to an abrupt halt the moment the wife comes home with the new baby. The changes that now become necessary are drastic. The baby needs round the clock attention. There are regular feeding and nappy changing sessions throughout the day *and* night, so you are tired because you don't get an uninterrupted night's sleep. If you are breastfeeding, you feel even more tired, but you still have to get up the next time the baby cries. No more lie-ins, no more leisurely mornings, no more days off. You have to learn about the baby, why it cries, what it needs, how to calm it down when it won't sleep.

All the everyday tasks and activities like going to the supermarket or popping out to the post office or shopping in a department store now need to be organized around the baby's feeding and sleeping time. Where before you could just get up and go whenever you felt like it, you now need to take all these new factors into consideration. Everything takes a lot longer because you need to get the baby ready. You are less mobile when you are pushing a pram or negotiating crowded pavements with a pushchair, but the real challenge arises when you are trying to go by bus! You need to be a female Houdini, taking the baby out of the chair once you are at the bus stop, folding the pushchair with one hand, heaving it up the steps, trying to wangle it into the compartment for pushchairs (still with only one hand), and now you could really do with an extra pair of hands to take some change out of your purse for the fare. Then getting off a few stops later, baby in one arm, getting the pushchair out of the storage compartment and onto the pavement, unfolding the chair with one hand, putting baby back into the pushchair, and then finally queuing up inside the post office to send off the parcel for your mother's birthday. Then back to the bus stop, taking baby out of the pushchair, folding the pushchair with one hand, and so on, until you are back home, feeling as if you had just fought World War Three all by yourself. You feel exhausted because you did not get much sleep last night and you would like nothing better than to sit down and have a cat nap for half an hour, but now the baby cries; it's feeding time again!

To a large extent, your own needs and wishes are becoming secondary. Even with more and more men helping their wives with the baby, the changes to the couple's life are considerable. Most parents, however, are able to get through these years reasonably well, especially if there is good support between partners and the possibility of occasional relief by leaving the child with a babysitter every once in a while.

However, problems can occur if there are additional difficulties with the child, for example if the child suffers from an illness or if the child is difficult. A client of mine, let's call her Jane, is a single mother in her early twenties, who suffered from panic attacks whenever she was outside the house. She had never had any problems before the child was born, but had noticed how the fear had developed over a period of two years. Her little daughter Francesca was a lively child, quite wilful and demanding, whereas Jane was a shy and retiring person who would have preferred to have someone else make decisions for her. She had been coping with the help of her mother when the baby was little but was experiencing difficulties now the child was able to walk and speak and her mother had to go back to work.

Jane felt that being a mother was getting on top of her. She became more and more fearful of going out after having had her first panic attack just as she was about to cross a road with her daughter in the pushchair. When she finally came to see me, she told me that she now needed to employ a great deal of will-power to force herself to go out at all.

She came to see me for seven sessions of analytical hypno-therapy during which we looked at how her changed status had affected her. When Francesca began to walk and talk and to explore her environment, it became clear very quickly who had the upper hand. Jane was often unable to get her little daughter to do what she wanted her to do; Francesca was simply the stronger personality when it came to a show-down. Occasion-ally Jane would scream at her daughter in sheer frustration which resulted in Francesca starting to cry. This in turn made Jane feel guilty and like a bad mother, so she would give in to Francesca once again.

Francesca categorically refused to be strapped into her push-chair when they went outdoors, so Jane, after a few feeble attempts, had given up and allowed her to sit in the chair without the belts fastened around her. One day when Jane was in the middle of crossing a road, Francesca jumped out of her chair and started running away. Jane, weighed down by shop-ping bags around each wrist and having to manoeuvre the chair, yelled for Francesca to stop and ran after her. She was so angry that she insisted on Francesca being strapped into the chair then, but the next day when the child was playing up, she gave in again. It was then that she started getting very apprehensive and nervous about being outside. Her anxiety became worse as time went by until, in the end, she preferred not to leave the house at all if she could avoid it.

During her hypnotherapy sessions, Jane began to understand that she needed to take control of home life because, after all, she was the adult. She also came to realize that being firm and setting limits has nothing to do with being a bad mother, even if the child protested. As Jane began to gain confidence, she was introduced to new options of dealing with her daughter. As her old methods were obviously not working, we were now trying out different ways of dealing with difficult situations such as getting Francesca to go to sleep or getting her to accept the pushchair straps.

In the past, Jane used to get Francesca ready for bed, read her a story and then try and leave the room. This sometimes worked, but only for about ten minutes. Francesca would then call and insist on being read another story and on Jane getting into bed with her until she fell asleep. The whole process took hours. Often, Francesca was up until very late in the evening so that Jane ended up with virtually no time to herself.

I suggested that Jane try out a new approach. Once Francesca was changed into her pyjamas, Jane would tell her not to go to bed under any circumstances but to keep on playing in her room. She, Jane, was going to be in the kitchen and would come and look in on Francesca later on. This worked very satisfactorily. When Jane went in to look how Francesca was doing, she would often find her curled up in bed, fast asleep, or the child was so tired that she would let Jane take her to bed quite willingly.

With new-found confidence, Jane also learnt to be firmer in other situations, explaining to Francesca why something needed to be done, for example being strapped into the seat, and calmly and firmly insisting on it by doing it, in spite of initial protests. After only a few times of Jane being firm, Francesca stopped making a fuss. As Jane was taking control of her new position as mother, her panic attacks faded very quickly. She felt more confident and was much calmer with her daughter, which in turn resulted in Francesca becoming an easier child.

Fear through trauma

When something dramatic happens in our lives, we can sometimes be left with an emotional scar, and this scar can often be a fear or phobia. If you have ever been burgled, you will know how the initial shock leaves you with a lingering fear of the same thing happening again. As you approach your house, you find yourself worrying about what you will find when you get to your front door. You are uneasy when you are in your flat because someone else has been in it and been through your things. You may even have problems sleeping because you keep listening for any unusual sounds at night.

When you have had an accident with your car, you may find that you become very anxious about driving again. When you have fallen off a horse and hurt yourself, you may be reluctant to get back into the saddle. When something goes wrong, when you are attacked or you get hurt, physically or emotionally, you can end up with a fear that lasts way past the original event.

This can happen, but it does not have to. Some people, through character or disposition, can deal with physical or emotional trauma better than others. Where one person can shrug off a mishap, another person may find themselves grappling with it for a long time. In some instances, a traumatic event can result in a life-long fear of situations that resemble the original event.

There are several factors that will determine whether lasting fear develops after trauma. One is, as mentioned before, the type of personality you are and what your natural resistance to stress is. Another factor is your general attitude towards problems and difficulties. This attitude is the result of past experiences and learning processes you have developed throughout the years. The state of mind you were in when the trauma occurred and how others reacted to what happened to you are also of importance.

Sometimes we can suffer from a fear or phobia without remembering the original trauma. All we know is that we hate water, but we have forgotten that this is because we fell into a pond as a child. We may be aware that we detest sex, but we do not remember that this is because we were sexually molested as a youngster. Traumatic memories can be repressed into the depths of the subconscious mind in order to prevent us from falling apart. But repressed memories always leave a visible trace, and this trace is often a fear.

A client of mine, Peter, had stopped driving his car after he had a near collision with a motorbike rider. Peter had approached a junction in town when he saw a motorbike rider lose his balance, the bike falling sideways and bike and rider sliding towards his car which, at this point, was stationary. Bike and rider slithered into the side of the car, but without too much of an impact. The biker got up almost instantly and seemed unharmed. Peter got out of the car and spoke to the man to make sure he was not hurt and to see if he needed any assistance, but the man assured him that he was not hurt. In the end,

Peter drove off, parked his car and didn't use it again for the next three years. What had happened here?

Peter came to see me because things had started getting out of hand. Not only was he afraid to drive his car, but he was now also frightened of going on a bus or on the underground. He said that he kept thinking that something might happen, either to him or someone else. When he was in the underground station, he had to stay well away from the edge of the platform in case someone pushed him from behind and he fell onto the rails. Or he would be haunted by images of someone else falling or being pushed onto the rails. Afterwards, he was not sure whether these images were real or imagined, whether an accident had indeed occurred or whether he had just been wrapped up in a fantasy. The only thing he knew for sure was that he was too frightened to go back into a tube station.

When Peter came to consult me he felt that his life was was ruled by fears. He could not go about easily, being unable to drive his own car or use public transport. He was not only severely limited in his mobility, but he was also worried about his state of mental health. Was he going mad, not being able to tell whether an accident had really occurred or whether he had just imagined it?

At first, Peter's case seemed baffling. The accident with the bike rider had been relatively harmless. Peter just happened to be there, but he had not caused the accident. The biker had got away with a shock, and Peter had been able to see for himself that the biker was unharmed. Not a drop of blood had been shed. And yet, this particular incident seemed to have triggered off his phobia of driving and ultimately his phobia of buses and the underground.

Peter insisted that the biker may have *seemed* all right, but maybe he wasn't. I began to see a tentative connection between this statement and the fearful thoughts that always went through his head while he was waiting for buses and trains. There seemed to be a conflict between whether what he saw was real or imagined. As this conflict was already established when the accident happened, I decided to go further back in time to see how it had originally come about.

I regressed Peter to his childhood where he remembered quite a few instances tha began to shed light on his fears. He remembered a time at school when he fell as he was running, grazing his shin. Even though the wound was hardly visible, with only a slight trickle of blood, he had great problems with the leg later on, and it took more than a year for him to regain the full use of that leg.

Then there were other memories of deaths that had occurred while he was a child. His favourite uncle had contracted cancer, and Peter went to see him in hospital with his mother. The uncle looked poorly, and the doctors had only given him a few more weeks to live. But instead of dying, the uncle recovered, much to Peter's surprise and delight, and lived another fifteen years. And then suddenly, even though he looked fit and healthy, he was struck down by cancer again and died within two weeks.

Another memory was that of visiting his grandmother in hospital. Sitting by her bed, the grandmother pointed out another patient on the ward, a young man, who looked quite well and was walking about, talking to people. She said that this patient was not receiving any treatment because he only had a short time to live. When Peter returned the following week, the man had died.

There were a few more similar memories, but I think the above examples illustrate the case sufficiently. Peter had learnt to accept that appearances can be deceptive. His only slightly grazed leg turned out to be quite a serious problem. His apparently dying uncle recovered and then, apparently healthy, died. The patient on the ward *looked* OK, but then died. So when the biker crashed into Peter's car, Peter's subconscious mind made that old connection again – the biker *looked* all right, but that was probably just as deceptive as all the previous times!

What aggravated the situation further was the fact that Peter had just separated from a longstanding girlfriend when the accident occurred. This meant that he was already in a state of emotional upset and the accident was only the last straw to trigger off a spiral of anxiety.

Once Peter had made all these connections on a conscious level, his phobias disappeared, and he was able to go back to driving his car and using public transport.

When a trauma occurs, it seems as if the upsetting experience becomes encapsulated in your mind, not allowing other, more positive experiences to modify the emotional content of the trauma. If you get bitten by a dog and if this event becomes locked into your mind as a trauma, it won't make any difference to you how many dogs there are who are friendly and harmless; your view of dogs remains negative and you cross onto the other side of the pavement when you see one. The trauma makes you act *as if all dogs were dangerous.*

In order to overcome these automatic fear-reactions that can (but don't have to) become established after trauma, there are quite a few methods which can be employed – you will read about these later in the book. But even though the techniques vary, they all have one thing in common: they change the subconscious message that is playing in your mind when a fear-inducing situation arises from negative to positive.

Fear through repressed anger

In the previous section, we looked at the way fear can evolve from trauma. Even though the underlying reason may not always be immediately apparent to an outside observer or even to the sufferer him- or herself, it is nevertheless very logical when we look at it on a symbolic level.

The pattern becomes more intricate and therefore less tangible when we experience fears that are caused by seemingly unrelated forces. This can make experiencing the fear even more worrying. When you are afraid of cats because someone threw a cat in your face once, you may not be happy to find yourself stuck with a phobia, but at least you don't feel you are going insane. When, however, you are twenty-five years old, fit and healthy, but you cannot move about outdoors without clinging to another person or holding on to a rail because you are afraid of falling over, and when there is no obvious reason for this fear, you may very well feel that you are going mad.

These awful sensations of helplessness and vulnerability are only surpassed by the feelings you go through the moment a panic attack descends on you. The sensations that occur at that moment can be so forceful that they show the same physical symptoms as a heart attack. I have treated several clients who had been taken into hospital as an emergency a few times in the past, only to be told that they had 'only' had a panic attack.

When such a thing happens, the standard medical procedure is still very often to prescribe tranquillizers. Unfortunately, this does not solve the problem. It will help sedate the patient, but often to a degree where they feel like a zombie and are unable to function normally and think clearly. In addition, the patient also runs the danger of becoming dependent on the tranquillizers (see also p. 29).

Moreover, taking the tranquillizers does not resolve the underlying cause of the panic attacks. This means that when you finally come off the tablets, the likelihood of a relapse is considerable.

Martha has four children, all boys, two of whom are from her husband's first marriage. Those two older boys are rebellious and will not listen to Martha ('You're not our real mother *anyway!*'), the third boy is very slow-witted and needs a lot of support, and the youngest child is hyperactive and creates havoc unless he is supervised constantly. Martha's husband Fred is, as she says, 'useless'. He keeps out of it all. When his two boys call Martha names, he ignores it; when they disobey Martha, he does not support her by insisting they do as they are told. As Martha says, 'Fred plays dead so he doesn't have to get involved.'

Martha is an agile, petite 45-year-old with bags of energy who keeps her chaotic family together as best she can, but the moment she steps outside the house she becomes totally helpless. She can only walk along with the aid of a stick and always has to have someone to accompany her because she is afraid she will have a panic attack and faint and fall to the ground. On particularly bad days, she cannot even leave the house, and this worries her because it means that if those symptoms persisted she would soon be unable to run her own household. The one positive side-effect that came out of Martha's phobia was that Fred could no longer keep out of it all – he had to do the shopping now and would drive her on those days when she could not bear to walk around outside (see also the section on secondary gain, p. 44).

When we started unravelling Martha's present situation we found that she had a lot of understanding for her children. She was very caring and acknowledged that the older boys needed to adapt to the fact that they had a new mother, and she also

understood that the two younger children had their own particular needs through their handicaps. She was trying to be
patient with all of them because she wanted to be a good
mother. She swallowed it when the older boys were rude; she
accepted it when the smaller ones damaged something; she did
not insist on her instructions being followed. The only person
she would have a go at sometimes was her husband, but since
he did not react, she did not insist with him either.

This was going on day in, day out. Even though Martha did
all the work, her family ignored her.

At first, Martha was reluctant to admit that she was angry
about it. She felt she should not resent her family, on the
contrary − if only she could understand them better, their
relationship would improve. Over the years, rather than dealing
with her anger, Martha had done her best to suppress it.
Whenever she felt angry, she felt guilty because a good mother
shouldn't be angry with her children, and a good wife should
not nag her husband. So she kept on suppressing her anger.

Unfortunately, suppressing it doesn't make it go away. On
the contrary suppressed anger starts building up inside, creating
tension, and when the level of tension gets too high, it needs to
be released. As you won't allow it to come out in its proper
place, it has to come out somewhere else, and that is the
moment when you have a panic attack.

As Martha systematically learnt to deal with her family in a
firmer and more constructive way, her confidence began to
build and she started feeling better and less afraid of going
outside. As she took control of her situation at home, she learnt
to insist on being treated with respect and taken notice of. In
this way, she reduced her inner pressure − she was actively
dealing with every situation as it came along, rather than letting
things ride as she used to do before. Tension was no longer
allowed to build up inside, so there was no need for explosive
releases, and gradually the panic attacks lost their strength and
eventually vanished.

Emotional build-up can occur in all contexts: constant hassle
at work, parents who interfere or put you down, a partner who
constantly lets you down and so on. Fears are your warning
signal that you need to revise the way you live your life, and
the more you ignore the warning signal, the louder it is going

to sound inside you. Switching off the warning signal by popping a pill makes as much sense as switching off your burglar alarm without checking whether there is a burglar or not. The only difference is that burglar alarms often go off for inconsequential reasons – panic attacks never do!

Fear as part of the Pre-Menstrual Syndrome (PMS)

PMS was originally known as PMT, Pre-Menstrual Tension, as coined by Dr Frank in 1931. As further research was undertaken into this phenomenon, it turned out that there were many more physical and emotional symptoms besides tension that can accompany the time before a period for some women. As a consequence, the term was changed to Pre-Menstrual *Syndrome*, to encompass the variety of symptoms that can occur.

We speak of PMS when we are describing symptoms which regularly occur before menstruation, but not before ovulation, with a complete absence of symptoms after menstruation for a minimum of seven days. PMS only affects women of childbearing age.

Apart from numerous and often unpleasant physical symptoms, the time before women start their period can also involve changes on an emotional level. These emotional symptoms range from nervous tension to mood swings, anxiety, agoraphobia, irritability, depression, disorientation, confusion, crying and tremors and shakes. Depending on how severely the woman is affected by the emotional symptoms, her behaviour can change quite considerably through the negative emotions she experiences. Some women find that they become agoraphobic when they are premenstrual, others experience heightened anxiety on a general level. As a consequence, these women find that they are less efficient at work or at home; they feel depressed and just want to withdraw.

The menstrual cycle is monitored by a control centre in the brain, the hypothalamus. The hypothalamus also controls a number of other functions, amongst them the body's water balance, appetite, weight, mood and the sleep rhythm. This explains why, when the menstrual cycle is disturbed, for example by a deficiency of a particular hormone, other functions are upset as well, such as water balance, weight or mood.

If you are in any doubt whether your anxiety is due to PMS, keep a diary over the next three months (see also Chapter 3, p. 82). Mark the days of your period and check when the anxiety or agoraphobia sets in, and also note when the fear ends and when your next period starts. If you find that the end of your fear coincides with the onset of your next menstruation, you can be sure that there is a connection.

Men do not experience changes in hormone levels. Male sex hormones are on an even keel every single day, whereas women's hormones vary throughout the month.

During a normal menstrual cycle, four different sex hormones are produced in women – follicle stimulating hormone (FSH), luteinizing hormone (LH), oestrogen and progesterone.

Both follicle stimulating hormone and luteinizing hormone act on the ovaries. The follicle stimulating hormone stimulates the formation of little rings of cells (follicles) which house the immature egg. Luteinizing hormone is released at mid-cycle and helps burst the ripened follicle and discharge the egg cell, a process known as *ovulation*. Luteinizing hormone is also involved in causing new cells to form at the site of the burst follicle, and these cells in turn produce progesterone.

Oestrogen is a steroid hormone which is produced mainly by the ovaries. It is responsible for the development of breasts and other sexual characteristics in puberty, and it is also responsible for the production of fertile cervical mucus, the opening of the cervix and building up of blood in the lining of the uterus in preparation for a fertilized egg.

Progesterone, like oestrogen, is a steroid hormone, and it is secreted by the ovaries in the second part of the cycle. It helps the fallopian tubes contract more forcefully so that the egg cell can be swept to the womb more easily. Progesterone also changes the consistency of the vaginal discharge from a watery fluid into a thick, sticky mucus which would prevent further sperm from entering the womb once an egg was fertilized.

During menstruation, oestrogen levels rise and reach a peak towards the end of the period and a few days after. Then oestrogen output begins to fall until ovulation occurs, at which stage both oestrogen and progesterone levels begin to rise, reaching their peak about a week before onset of the next menstruation.

There are indications that a low level of progesterone may be responsible for some PMS symptoms. When, during pregnancy, menstruation stops and the blood level of progesterone rises, women with pre-menstrual syndrome lose their symptoms.

Progesterone also plays a part in the regulation of the blood sugar level. The blood sugar is maintained by eating carbohydrates which are present in starchy foods such as flour, potatoes and rice, and by eating sugars. If the blood sugar level drops too low, for example after a long spell without food, there is a danger of loss of consciousness or, in extreme cases, death.

To prevent this from happening, a regulating mechanism in the body is activated which causes a sudden burst of adrenalin which mobilizes sugar stored in the cells and passes it into the blood so that the blood sugar level is balanced again. However, when sugar is taken from the cells, it is replaced by water, and this is what you experience as water retention, bloating and weight gain during periods.

Progesterone is involved in this regulating mechanism, and if there is too little progesterone before menstruation, the mechanism comes into action much earlier; in other words, the negative effects of low blood sugar (moodiness, anxiety and so on) happen more quickly, approximately three hours after having eaten. It is therefore advisable to make sure you eat small portions at three hour intervals to ensure that you can stay on an emotionally even keel.

Make sure you always have some emergency supplies of food with you in case you are away from home or the shops. It is very important to keep to the three-hour-routine throughout the whole cycle, not just before your period. (For more information on blood sugar, see p. 33.)

Supervising your food intake is one way of dealing with PMS symptoms. Another form of treatment that is available is that of administering progesterone. Unfortunately, oral progesterone has proved to be ineffective in combating PMS; instead pessaries, suppositories or injections are normally used, usually from the time of ovulation until the onset of menstruation every month. However, the time at which progesterone is given needs to be tailormade to each individual woman so that medication can be started *before* the onset of symptoms. It is therefore important to monitor initially very carefully by way of charts at what stage in the cycle the symptoms start appearing. Also, there is a considerable difference in the absorption of progesterone by individuals which will have an effect on how many pessaries or suppositories you will have to take a day.

Effects of both the dietary and hormonal treatment, if applied properly, can be transforming. Women who had spent year after year feeling miserable and anxious for two weeks out of four reported that they felt like they had been given a new lease of life.

Fear through withdrawal from tranquillizers

Over recent years, there have been an increasing number of newspaper reports concerning legal action taken against pharmaceutical firms who produce tranquillizers. In 1989, a steering committee of solicitors, representing sixty-four Scottish legal firms, began investigating the side-effects of the benzodiazepine family of tranquillizers, including Ativan and Valium. Even though the precise number of potential claimants was still unknown, the Law Society of Scotland said it had received more than 2,000 enquiries.

Benzodiazepines are principally used to treat anxiety, and they are referred to as anxiolytics, anxiolytic-sedatives, tranquillizers or 'tranks'. They have four main functions – sedative, anti-anxiety, muscle relaxant and anti-convulsant.

Benzodiazepines

alprazolam (Xanax)
bromazepam (Lexotan)
chlordiazepoxide (Librium, Tropium)
chlormezanone (Trancopal)
clobazam (Frisium)
clorazepate dipotassium (Tranxene)
diazepam (Alupram, Atensine, Diazemuls, Evacalm, Solis,

   Stesolid, Tensium, Valium)
ketazolam (Anxon)
lorazepam (Almazine, Ativan)
medazepam (Nobrium)
oxazepam (Oxanid)
prazepam

Benzodiazepines are 'downers'. They calm you down, and in larger doses they send you to sleep. As benzodiazepines impair brain function, they have a debilitating effect on mental and physical performance. The side-effects include drowsiness, light-headedness, lack of coordination and difficulty in walking which can make it problematic or impossible to work or drive a car while on the pills. Some people have also reported suffering from agoraphobia when they were on these drugs. This is ironic, considering that the drugs were initially prescribed to combat anxiety, only to leave the patient with another fear instead.

   Although they are 'downers', benzodiazepines can also produce opposite effects in some people. Instead of calming them down, the drugs act as 'uppers', and the person becomes excited and aggressive, in some cases even suicidal.

   It has also been shown that benzodiazepines increase the effects of alcohol and can increase the effects of other drugs such as sleeping pills, anti-depressants or barbiturates which are often prescribed in conjunction with tranquillizers.

   However, the real problems start when a user tries to come off these drugs. Benzodiazepines have an effect on the brain and they produce addiction within a relatively short time (four to six weeks) if taken regularly. If you then stop taking these tranquillizers suddenly, you develop severe anxiety, tension and panic attacks, nausea, trembling, palpitation, sweating and difficulty in sleeping, and these are only a *few* of the symptoms. The National Tranquillizer Advice Centre (TRANX), who sadly had to give up their work due to underfunding, gave a list of *110 symptoms* that can occur on withdrawal! In extreme cases, you can feel depersonalized (like a 'zombie'), become confused and end up with a nervous breakdown or delusions and hallucinations. You can feel as if you are going mad.

   As there are still doctors who are unfamiliar with the fact that these symptoms are caused by chemical changes due to withdrawal, they end up prescribing more tranquillizers or antidepressants, thus starting the vicious circle all over again.

Here are two reports from people who have come off tranquillizers.

> I have now been drug-free for 11 months and I am beginning to live a 'normal' life. I have just returned to work full-time, and the other great achievement is that I have just passed my driving test. This time last year when I was a shaking wreck, unable to move outside of my home, afraid to be left alone, I would never have believed that my life could be so different only 12 months later.
>
> Sometimes I get very anxious and my heart races for no reason, other days my head aches and I feel sick and dizzy, and occasionally for no reason I get very depressed. I am sure these are just further withdrawal symptoms but as I have just moved I don't really want to go to a new doctor just yet who I'm afraid may just suggest that it's all due to anxiety, as many other doctors have done in the past.

Another person who had come off Librium three months previously:

> When I become over-tired, which is often, I easily get palpitations which are upsetting, and I find difficulty sleeping. When tense I become very conscious of my heart thumping and I have difficulty breathing in a natural relaxed way. I also make sudden 'jumps' in my sleep which wake me up with a fright. These are symptoms I experienced while on Valium.

These withdrawal symptoms can last *months*, rather than just weeks as some doctors seem to think. Ignorance about this basic fact results in aggravating the situation, as described by a client:

> I have been taking Valium (or its equivalent) for 10 years — they were originally prescribed for tension headaches — and I have been through the full gambit of psychiatrists and psychologists during that time, none of whom could help and none of whom would accept benzodiazepines could have very much to do with my condition.
>
> I stopped taking Valium, having reduced from 15mg per day, and actually felt fine — very few withdrawal symptoms etc. But suddenly, I started having night-time palpitations, missed heart beats and a constantly rapid heart beat. My doctor prescribed betablockers which I couldn't function on — they knocked me out, so in

desperation he put me *back* on 6 mg Valium. I was absolutely terrified and very panicky – not for one moment thinking that I could be suffering withdrawal – after all, the doctor had said it should only take THREE WEEKS!!

I am now *again* down to 2 mg a day. I am, at different times, suffering all the withdrawal symptoms you mention, plus a few others, the worst being the overwhelming feelings of panic towards any thought that comes into my head. I have to stop myself from rushing over to my son's school to make sure he is OK during the day etc. Also my concentration is bad and especially whilst I'm with other people, I feel as though I am unable to react to them. I feel as though I don't belong anywhere and go through periods of depression. *It's as though there is a transparent barrier around me. I can't get out and they can't get in.*

I have mentioned all these terrifying sensations to a psychiatrist who is trying to dig down much further and cannot believe that it is due to withdrawal. I feel as though I am trapped in the 'system', labelled 'Anxiety Neurosis' and nobody knows quite what to do with me. I felt rejected and frightened; after all, if they can't help me, who can?

In the US, the state of New York was the first to introduce strict controls on benzodiazepines. According to *The New York Times*, the programme began on January 1st 1989, restricting prescriptions to a one-month supply, with no automatic refills, and requiring one copy of each prescription filled to go to the state, the others remaining with the physician and the pharmacist. Health officials told the newspaper that the controls were necessary in order to identify physicians who prescribe the drugs too liberally and to shut down the 'pill mills' that sell prescriptions to addicts and teenagers. The National Institute of Drug Abuse has found that such abuse by addicts had doubled among adults from 3.1 per cent of all benzodiazepine prescriptions in 1980 to 7.1 per cent in 1985.

All this does not paint a pretty picture for anyone who has been taking tranquillizers and now wants to come off them, and it is sad that there is so little support for people who want to regain control of their life by taking the courageous step to leave their pills behind. On the other hand, it is necessary for patients to know that they are not going mad when they experience these frightening withdrawal symptoms, and that if they persist, they will ultimately be able to rid themselves of the pills *and* the withdrawal symptoms.

Tranquillizers *can* be useful if taken over a short period of time, but they can never constitute a true solution to any anxiety problem. Rather than just 'popping a pill', see a counsellor or a therapist to find out what is causing the anxiety. That way you can work through the underlying problem, and you don't end up having the problem of addiction on top of the problem of anxiety.

Fear through medical conditions, allergies and stimulants

If you suffer from any anxiety related condition, you should always check that this is not due to a physical or nutritional problem or to an excessive use of stimulants such as coffee, tea or nicotine. Even though these are not always the sole cause of the fear problem, they can in many cases exacerbate the fear to a considerable extent.

The two major medical conditions which can cause anxiety or panic are hypoglycaemia and hyperthyroidism.

Hypoglycaemia is a condition where the blood sugar level temporarily drops below normal. Glucose enables our body and brain to function normally; it gives us energy and keeps us awake and, indeed, alive. Were the blood sugar level to drop past a certain point, we would fall into a coma and ultimately die.

The blood sugar content is monitored by an internal bodily mechanism that monitors the rise and fall of blood sugar levels between an upper and a lower limit. Hypoglycaemia occurs when the blood sugar level falls below the lower limit, and this can be caused either by stress or by the intake of too much sugar. Sudden or chronic stress can cause a rapid depletion of sugar because of the increased demands on your system. You experience anxiety and confusion because your brain is not getting enough sugar *and* because of the adrenalin and cortisol that are flooding your system.

A similar thing happens when you eat too much sugar (and in particular refined sugar). In this case, the pancreas is forced to release a great amount of insulin to enable the excess sugar to be taken up by the cells. When you eat too much sugar, you initially experience a 'high', but this is followed by a rapid drop to a 'low' feeling after about half an hour, and it is this low feeling that coincides with a feeling of nervousness or fear.

You will find ways of dealing with hypoglycaemia on p. 158 in Chapter 3 of the book.

Hyperthyroidism (or thyrotoxicosis) is the other physical condition that is often associated with anxiety. The disease is found seven times more often in women than in men, and it often occurs in several family members. Hyperthyroidism is the result of either iodine deficiency causing goitre, or it can stem from a pathological process called autoimmunity in which the body's immune system generates autoantibodies that are harmful to the body's own tissues.

Hyperthyroidism typically begins with a gradual onset of symptoms such as increased nervousness and emotional instability (mood swings), associated with a fine tremor of the hands. The person feels warm and perspires easily, the pulse races, blood pressure goes up and the heart thumps. (All these symptoms also occur when you feel very frightened!) The excess of thyroid hormones leads to an increased rate of metabolism so that a person loses weight in spite of increased appetite. Often, there is also a swelling on the neck where the thyroid gland is located.

In many cases, hyperthyroidism can be successfully treated with medication that blocks the release of thyroid hormones. Another option is to surgically remove all but a small part of the thyroid in order to normalize hormone output.

Anxiety and panic can also be caused by an allergic reaction to certain foods or food additives. Knowledge about adverse reactions to foods has been applied over recent years to help people with disorders as diverse as headaches, lethargy, obesity, bowel disturbances, hyperactivity, depression and chronic anxiety.

Food allergies are not always easy to detect unless you have a straightforward, direct reaction as soon as you have eaten the food. A friend of mine had fainted several times after eating desserts until she discovered that she was allergic to nuts. In a case like that, it is easy to just eliminate the food in question, and as long as you stay away from it, you will be fine.

A problem occurs when you have a so-called *masked food allergy*. If you suffer from such an allergy, you find that you actually crave these allergenic foods and feel quite addicted to them. You may know someone who needs to eat chocolate every day; other people crave bread or dairy products, without realizing that it is these foods that negatively influence their well-being. The noxious effects of these allergenic foods only become visible when you stay off them for a day or so. You suddenly feel restless, irritable and disorientated, and this makes you feel anxious.

To find out how you can test for a masked food allergy, please refer to the section on nutrition (p. 159).

But it is not just the foods themselves that can cause allergies and consequently anxiety problems; nowadays, there are also preservatives and other additives that are to blame. The so-called Chinese Restaurant Syndrome, or Kwok's Quease, was discovered by Dr Robert Kwok who used to eat Chinese foods regularly. One day, while having a Chinese meal at a restaurant, Dr Kwok was gripped by a terrifying pain in the chest which felt like a heart attack, and he collapsed. The pain subsided after a short while but Dr Kwok was determined to get to the bottom of this sudden seizure. He finally found that he was allergic to *monosodium glutamate* which is often used by Chinese chefs to enhance the flavour of their dishes.

Other non-food substances that can be allergenic are gas, synthetic fibres, petrol fumes, tar, cosmetics, and household cleaners, to name just a few. If you suspect that you might be allergic to any of these substances and you are unable to test for incompatibility yourself, you might want to consult an allergy specialist or a kinesiologist who can test for you.

Last but not least on the list of detrimental foods are stimulants such as coffee, tea and nicotine. Over the last ten years there have been an increasing number of reports about the noxious side effects of caffeine. It is now linked to conditions like nervous tension, anxiety, insomnia, depression, tremors and shakes, headaches, and even heart disease.

Caffeine is found in coffee, tea (but not in herbal teas), cola beverages, chocolate, cocoa and some pain killers. The reason why an excessive intake of caffeine can induce anxiety is that it has a directly stimulating effect on the body. Firstly, it increases the level of norepinephrine in the brain, and this makes you feel more 'alert'. Secondly, it also works on your sympathetic nervous system by activating it *as if you were under stress.* This means that adrenalin is released which gives you a feeling of alarm.

Apart from causing or aggravating anxiety, caffeine also blocks the absorption of essential vitamins such as B1 and minerals such as zinc and iron. This can lead to an impaired resistance to infection, disturbed hormone production and disturbed mental function.

Nicotine is as strong a stimulant as caffeine. Because smoking constricts the blood vessels, the heart has to work a lot harder to pump the blood around your system. This means that not only do you run an increased risk of varicose veins, insomnia and heart problems, but you also create a situation where, with every single cigarette you smoke, you greatly increase the likelihood of experiencing anxiety through heightened physiological arousal.

Tips about reducing caffeine and nicotine intake can be found in the section on nutrition on pp. 162–4.

CONSCIOUS AND SUBCONSCIOUS PROCESSES

In the introduction to Chapter 1 of this book, I have already briefly described how an automatic fear response comes about. I would now like to go into more detail about the interplay between conscious and subconscious processes, as knowledge about these processes is fundamental to resolving trauma caused by or resulting in fear.

Both the conscious and the subconscious parts of our mind are necessary to allow us to function competently in everyday life. The conscious mind helps us make day-to-day decisions on a logical basis, whereas the subconscious mind is in charge of the sympathetic nervous system, controlling all involuntary bodily functions, as well as storing all our experiences in the form of memories. It is storing everything we have ever learned in the past, from doing up our shoelaces to using a pen, from driving a car to working a computer. Furthermore, the subconscious mind is the seat of intuition, ideas, attitudes, habits, self-image and the entire range of emotions.

As you can see, the subconscious mind has a considerably larger number of things to do than the conscious, and indeed, the conscious mind is said to take up only about five per cent of our mind, whereas the subconscious occupies ninety-five per cent. This of course means that not only are we not using a large proportion of our capacity, but it also means that our behaviour and our reactions are largely decided by components that are outside the reach of consciousness.

Remember the last time you made a conscious decision to pull yourself together over a certain matter, only to find that your feelings overruled you? You were determined to give up smoking, you gave yourself all the logical reasons why you should quit, but the sight of a pack of cigarettes proved too tempting to resist. You had decided to stay calm when broaching an annoying subject with your partner, but you still ended up yelling at her. You had meant to finally tackle this awkward job at the office, only to find you were postponing it yet again because you just could not face it after all. In all these examples, you can observe a struggle of rational mind versus irrational mind, and when the conscious and subconscious clash, it is always the subconscious that wins.

Even though the subconscious is the larger part, it is nevertheless the simpler part of the mind. It functions on the yes/no principle – either something happens or it doesn't; there is only black and white, there are no grey areas in between. The subconscious also works as an auto-pilot system. Responses are triggered automatically. As soon as a stimulus appears, the subconscious switches into gear. You see a photograph of a beautiful beach – your subconscious mind releases hormones into your body that make you feel good and relax. You watch a row between two people in a pub and your subconscious gives you signals of discomfort and you leave the pub. Because the subconscious works on auto-pilot, it functions very quickly and efficiently. The conscious mind, on the other hand, can deliberate and think in intricate ways, covering all the 'grey' areas, but this makes it less powerful and ultimately slower than the automatic reactions of the subconscious. So if you have low self-esteem (subconscious) and are deciding (conscious) to go for a higher ranking job, chances are that your subconscious negative view of yourself will sabotage your conscious endeavours. Either you find yourself postponing sending off your application form or you get so nervous that you flunk the interview.

It is only when your feelings (subconscious) are in harmony with your willpower (conscious) that you will get the results you are striving for (see also Vera Peiffer, *Positive Thinking*). So when you are stuck with an unwanted behaviour or reaction such as fear, you will need to change things on a subconscious level because this is where the fear, just like any other emotion, comes from. Changes on a conscious level are useless as long as the subconscious stays the same. *Willing* yourself to be unafraid only creates internal conflict and uses up a lot of valuable energy. If you are afraid of flying and force yourself to do it, you will know how exhausted you are at the end of the journey, and this exhaustion comes from trying to keep the lid on your fear. When you suffer from anxiety you will know how tired you feel all the time, simply because you have to pull yourself together so much just to get through the day.

The subconscious mind is always on our side, it works for us as a protector, trying to shield us from harm. In that sense, a fear reaction must be seen as a basically positive reaction against a supposed peril, and as such it is of course quite useful. But if the protective reaction is blocking us too often and too regularly, it also makes us weak. Because we are not tackling enough problems and we are facing too few challenges, our ability to cope is not being exercised enough and wastes away.

Because being afraid emanates from the subconscious, we can consciously recognize that it is silly to be afraid of speaking up at a meeting and at the same time be unable to stop being afraid. It is useless telling someone with a phobia to 'pull themselves together'. Pulling yourself together happens on a conscious level; it is a special effort of willpower which is supposed to solve a problem rationally. Unfortunately this is not the mental level the problem originates from, as we have seen. Any approach that intends to resolve fear will have to help bring about change in the subconscious mind. This means that a particular attitude in a person's mind has to change. When they feel useless, they need to experience that they can be useful; when they feel like a victim, they need to get in touch with their power; when they can only feel fear, they need to experience other, more active emotions such as anger. Before fears can go, the old attitudes need to go and be replaced by new and more productive ones.

There are a variety of techniques, either in form of self-help or therapy, that can be very useful in this context, and we shall have a look at them in Chapter 3 of the book.

PHYSICAL, MENTAL AND EMOTIONAL SYMPTOMS

How do you know that you are afraid? If you are not afraid right now, you may find it difficult to answer this question. Most people will describe fear as being situated in their stomach or belly area where it is producing unpleasant sensations ('butterflies'); other people will describe symptoms like sweaty hands, trembling knees and a pounding heart.

As we have seen, feelings are part of the subconscious part of the mind, and so are the involuntary bodily functions of the sympathetic nervous system. This system is responsible for processes like adjusting the pupils of the eye when the intensity of light changes, contracting the skin into goosebumps when we are cold (or afraid!) and regulating our day/night rhythm of sleeping and waking, to name but a few. All these bodily functions are directly interlinked with our emotional state, and with every change of emotion, no matter how slight, the finely balanced body mechanisms of blood chemistry change. This is necessary for the body to function at its optimum level at all times. When we have to concentrate hard, the body immediately releases certain transmitter substances which make us perform better; when we are happy, the brain releases endorphines which give us a high; when we are angry, adrenalin is pumped out and the heart beats faster to prepare us for action.

Just like all these other feelings, being afraid also results in changes on a physical level, and the greater the fear, the greater the physical changes. Depending on how strongly you experience your fear, you will be aware of some or all of the symptoms in the following list. Some of these symptoms are also visible to an outside observer.

Physical symptoms

hair	standing on end when fear-inducing situation arises
jaws	clenching of teeth; teeth grinding, also when asleep
throat	constricted feeling; inability to swallow; dryness in mouth; choking; speaking with a 'pressed' voice
shoulders/neck	tightness, sometimes 'locked' feeling; pain whilst moving; pain whilst sitting still; sensitivity to touch; stiffness; headaches through tension in these areas
back	see shoulders/neck. Also shooting or stabbing pains in the back region or across the back
breathing	irregular; shallow, only filling up the top half of the lungs because diaphragm is cramped up; hyperventilation which can occur with no apparent reason, resulting in dizziness and fear of fainting or falling over
heart	palpitations (heart racing for no apparent reason); 'claw' around the heart; tightness of chest, similar to feelings preceding a heart attack
stomach	'knotted' feeling, 'butterflies'; stomach noises; uncomfortably tight feeling resulting in loss of appetite; ulcers can develop when food is replaced by alcohol and/or cigarettes; nausea; fear of vomiting
bowels	negative changes in bowel functioning

such as constipation or diarrhoea; irritable bowel syndrome; needing to urinate more than usual

auto-immune system   tendency to catch any illness that is going around; greater likelihood of falling ill because of weakened resistance to viruses and other pathogenic agents; existing illnesses can become worse; wounds won't heal properly or take a very long time to heal. MS occurs only in people who are of an anxious disposition

menstruation   aggravated period pains; irregular periods or missed periods

twitches   which can go on over a prolonged period of time, then stop suddenly and recur at a later time

blushing

trembling   and shaking

tiredness   yawning a lot; lack of energy, no matter how long you have slept; general feeling of being run down

skin   eczema occurs or, if it already exists, gets worse; rashes; feelings of numbness

All these physical symptoms can occur as consequences of being afraid at a particular moment in time, or they can occur through prolonged exposure to fear-inducing situations or through unresolved events from the past that result in fearful reactions to everyday events.

As you are looking through the list of symptoms, you will realize that many of them could also be explained from a different angle. You can have constant headaches because you have a brain tumour or because you are allergic to cheese or wine; you can have diarrhoea because you have eaten something that was off; your back can ache because you have slipped a disc or because you do your typing sitting on an unsuitable chair. There are usually a variety of factors that could produce the above symptoms, so it is essential to check first of all whether there is a mechanical problem which is causing the physical discomfort before assuming that it is due to anxiety or stress. Once these physical or mechanical factors have been ruled out, there is every possibility that your problem is of a psychosomatic nature, that is to say that your physical problem is caused by an imbalance on the emotional side, and this imbalance can be caused by excessive or persistent fear.

However, the physical symptoms are only *one* aspect of experiencing fear. At the same time, there are also mental and emotional consequences, and they tend to exacerbate the original problem even further.

Mental and emotional symptoms

inability to concentrate	not taking anything in that you are listening to; having to re-read the same page many times
memory	deteriorating, not being able to recall simple, everyday things
racing around	physically and mentally; inability to relax and do nothing; feeling uncomfortable with meditation and yoga
fidgeting	inability to sit still; biting or picking nails; picking nose; pulling out hair
insecurity	inability to make decisions; avoiding taking responsibility
depression	not wanting to face the world any more; withdrawal from social life
aggressiveness	being overcritical; attacking at the slightest hint of complications; irritability
vulnerability	tearfulness; avoiding anything that could potentially create stress; feeling at the mercy of other people; being mistrustful; feeling persecuted; being overly self-critical
erratic behaviour	failing to do things in an orderly fashion; starting lots of things and not finishing anything; being gauche;

	making silly mistakes; making the same mistakes over and over again; trying to do everything at once
compulsive/obsessive behaviour	having recurring negative thoughts which cannot be stopped; having to have everything in apple-pie order all the time; exaggerated need for tidiness; checking and re-checking locks/water taps/cooker etc
feeling incompetent	apologizing a lot; putting yourself down
low frustration threshold	giving up very quickly when something doesn't produce expected results immediately
exaggerated expectations	of oneself and others
lack of motivation	apathy; loss of interest in anything that is not strictly necessary for everyday survival
speech	stuttering; stammering; hitching on certain words
sleep	disrupted; insomnia; nightmares; bedwetting in children
sex	impotence; premature ejaculation; vaginism; frigidity
detachment	feeling of being out of touch with yourself; feeling of not being yourself (depersonalization)
disorientation	losing your way easily

Unlike the physical symptoms, many of the mental and emotional symptoms that are listed here can be said to occur as a direct consequence of fear. They do not *all* have to emerge if you suffer from a fear-related problem, but whichever one of them does, you will certainly have to look at fear as being a strong contributory factor. In this context it is immaterial whether these mental and emotional symptoms have always existed in a person or whether they have come about later on in life – they always indicate the presence of fear in some shape or form.

SECONDARY GAIN

Nobody *likes* being afraid, but sometimes it can have its advantages. When a mother is strict and not very affectionate towards her children but becomes caring and gentle when her children are scared at night, then there is a positive side to being afraid. When a husband is generally a cold fish but becomes concerned and attentive every time his wife starts screaming when she sees a spider, then the spider phobia brings with it a definite beneficial side-effect, and the husband may find to his amazement that his house seems to have more and more spiders in it . . .

Whenever a symptom such as fear or an illness is used to bring about a desired reaction from the environment, we speak of secondary gain. You may possibly remember having used this ploy when you were a child and didn't want to go to school for one reason or another. You may have had an only *slightly* unpleasant feeling in your stomach, but you made out it was really bad so you were allowed to stay home. Or you may have prolonged an illness by not admitting that you were better so that you got attention for a bit longer – in other words, you were using your illness to attain a particular goal.

Whether you are using an illness or a fear to achieve a particular aim doesn't really make a difference. What you are doing in either case is to gain attention in an indirect way by manipulating others with your symptom. You are doing this because you don't believe you can get the attention any other way.

This doesn't mean that the fear is not genuine or that the person who has the fear is not suffering – on the contrary. Once the fear is well established it can cause the person a lot of aggravation, especially when it stops having the desired effect of attracting attention. What gives it away is that when these people finally seek help, it is often their partner who urges them to do so, while the client him- or herself is adamant that no one can help them; they are 'just coming along to do their partner a favour'. They are afraid to let go of their fear because if they do, they feel they are giving up the means to make other people be affectionate or attentive towards them. Their fear endows them with a certain power over others, and they are most reluctant to let go of that power.

A lady client came to see me, initally escorted by her husband. She was suffering from severe agoraphobia and was unable to leave the house unless accompanied by her husband. This meant that all the shopping and any errands had to be done after her husband came home from work or on a Saturday when he was off work. During the day she would stay indoors, doing the housework and occasionally having a friend around. All this was related to me by the husband while his wife was sitting in her chair like a school girl who had been summoned to the head mistress's office for misconduct. In the end, I had to send the husband out of the office because he would not let his wife answer for herself.

When Irene told her story it was quickly confirmed that in her marriage her husband Peter was the dominant partner who would criticize easily, praise rarely and would generally show very little affection. Irene's agoraphobia had started in the third year of their marriage. She had always been quite shy, and her husband's permanent criticism had made her even more so, losing any confidence she had so that her self-esteem became very low. There were times when she didn't want to go out because she felt depressed and anxious. Her husband withdrew even more emotionally, telling her to pull herself together and not be in such a 'mood' all the time or he would leave her.

The final blow for Irene came when she found a note in Peter's coat which indicated that he was seeing someone else. She was very shocked and felt that her whole world had come crashing down around her. It was at this point that she began to feel an increase in anxiety about leaving the house. As she could no longer do the shopping, go to the post office or the doctor's and dentist's by herself, her husband had to come straight home from work and either do things for her or go with her. Irene also become anxious about being in the house on her own, so he had to spend a lot of time with her over the weekend. Irene just couldn't be left alone at all; Peter was required to be in constant attendance unless he was working.

As you read this account you will no doubt have understood the nature of the gain that Irene derived from her phobia — on the one hand, she was limiting any spare time Peter might have to see the other woman, and on the other hand she made sure he spent a lot of time with her and gave her some attention. Even though Peter was still not any nicer to her, at least no other women would have him! It was nearly like an act of revenge on Irene's part. She wanted to keep her husband, but she also wanted to punish him for his inconsiderate behaviour.

It is not always easy to assess the extent to which a fear is being consciously used to manipulate and to what extent the fear is genuine. There is almost certainly always a large percentage of real fear involved, and in many cases people are unaware, on a conscious level, that their fear is also fulfilling a secondary function for them.

It can be difficult to treat people with a fear that is anchored in a secondary gain system because the client will either not co-operate or will seemingly go along with the treatment but find excuses every time they are asked to do homework such as jotting down what is happening during the day, at which point the fear occurs and so on. These clients tend to have a very low level of motivation and often drop out. It they stick with the treatment, they often give the impression of being determined to prove that nobody can help them, which is their way of saying that they don't want to let go of the problem.

I am glad to say that in years of practising as a therapist I have come across very few clients like that.

2. Different Fears

Having looked at the principles that govern fear as well as the causes and effects, we now come to the qualitative and quantitative differences between various kinds of fear; in other words, we shall be looking at the different levels and the different categories of fear. Naturally, there are no clear cut limits to where apprehension ends and anxiety starts, and in that sense, categorization is by necessity artificial.

Fears are not steady all the time; they can vary in strength and frequency from day to day, depending on your overall mood and on what else is happening around you. This can mean that one day your fear is nearly unbearable whereas on a 'good' day it is quite manageable.

I will describe each section in as much detail as possible to give you the chance to compare my outline against your own experience to determine what section your particular fear comes under. You may also find it useful to think for a moment about a time when your particular fear was at its worst – this will help you find the right category more easily.

DIFFERENT LEVELS

In the following, I will use a grading system to denote the intensity with which fear occurs. The scale goes from zero to ten. *Please note that this is not a scientific scale.*

Every person experiences fear in their own individual way. This can be compared to the different pain thresholds people have. If you put someone's arm in a vice and told them to let you know at what point they started feeling pain, you would get very different accounts. Even though you can measure scientifically the degree to which you close the vice around the arm, some people will stop you much earlier than others.

Chances are that an anxious person will experience pain at an earlier stage than a confident person. This is because fear exacerbates the perception of pain; the two are closely linked. So in this example, we can measure the width of the vice, but we cannot measure the mental and emotional state the subject is in. The only indication we have of the subject's mental and emotional state is their own perception of it, that is their indication of when they begin to experience a sensation of pain.

And even that indication will vary from day to day. A woman who is about to have her period may be more sensitive to pressure on her skin than on other days of her cycle; a man who has been drinking the previous night may be more sensitive to pain than when he is well rested and sober.

The same variations occur of course within the fear experience. The only thing we could measure scientifically here would be the physical responses like skin tension, blood pressure and so on, but when you have a spider phobia, the last thing you want to think about is getting your stop watch out and counting your pulse rate while one of your little friends is crawling across the carpet! So, again, the only thing you have to go by is *your personal perception* of fear and how it affects your body.

You have read in a previous chapter what the physical signs of fear are, and no matter how shocked you are, you can usually recall afterwards what bodily symptoms you experienced *while* you were afraid or *shortly after* the fearful moment has passed.

In my description of the various levels on our fear scale I will therefore take into consideration these physical symptoms, and they should give you a broad guideline as to the approximate level you are at. Knowing your level can then help you to decide whether you are likely to need professional help with your fear or whether you might be able to overcome the problem through self-help techniques.

I will be using the scale in later parts of the book, so you may want to put a bookmark between the pages here so that you can refer back to the scale whenever you need to.

THE 10-POINT FEAR SCALE

LEVEL 0 (no fear)
    physical symptoms: calm, relaxed
    mental symptoms: calm, relaxed, awake
    emotional symptoms: peaceful
    behaviour: rational, organized, unhurried, calm and collected

Comments: Nobody is at this state all the time. Most people only come down to this level of comfort when they are asleep, meditating or when they are on holiday and there are no outside pressures at all.

LEVEL 1
    physical symptoms: calm, relaxed
    mental symptoms: fleeting thoughts of minor worries which do not leave a perceivable trace; very good concentration
    emotional symptoms: calm
    behaviour: rational, organized, unhurried, calm and collected

Comments: Not often achieved unless you feel very much together and are a truly easy-going person.

LEVEL 2
    physical symptoms: calm, slight feelings of a 'buzz' in the body
    mental symptoms: repeated thoughts about worries, very slightly distracted sometimes
    emotional symptoms: slight feeling of unease, often still below consciousness level
    behaviour: rational and organized

Comments: A good, comfortable level which many people can achieve most of the time.

LEVEL 3

physical symptoms:	slight feeling of unease in stomach area
mental symptoms:	worrying, going over a problem repeatedly in your mind
emotional symptoms:	feeling of unease that persists and is noticed by you
behaviour:	rational and organized, concentration is still good, even though mind wanders off sometimes

Comments: With physical symptoms beginning to show, this is the start of the 'discomfort level'. Not serious though, and easily managed.

LEVEL 4

physical symptoms:	unease in stomach, slight tension in neck/back/shoulders
mental symptoms:	worrying beginning to affect performance slightly
emotional symptoms:	clear feeling of unease, apprehensive
behaviour:	still rational, making occasional mistakes through lack of concentration

Comments: As performance is beginning to be affected, some attention is needed to bring down the stress level. Easily managed with self-help concepts.

LEVEL 5

physical symptoms:	as in level 4, but also involuntary clenching of teeth (pain in jaw area), possibility of headaches, breathing is often irregular
mental symptoms:	problems relaxing, deteriorating memory, sleeping problems
emotional symptoms:	feeling stressed, mood swings
behaviour:	still mostly rational, but restless and a bit disorganized, irrational decisions when mood is low, but still able to control fear rationally

Comments: At this point, it is time to take positive action – this is where your fear can become a real problem if you don't watch it. You definitely need to control your stress.

LEVEL 6
physical symptoms:	as in level 5, but also possibility of occasional problems with stomach/bowels
mental symptoms:	occasional feelings of confusion
emotional symptoms:	feeling anxious and nervous, awareness that something is wrong
behaviour:	rushed, often irrational, clumsy, fidgeting

Comments: The fear has become a real problem now because there are the first signs of 'not being yourself'. With a lot of commitment, you may still be able to get rid of the fear by yourself.

LEVEL 7
physical symptoms:	as in level 6, but also possibility of dizziness, constricted throat ('pressed' voice) and palpitations
mental symptoms:	confused, disorientated, feeling you cannot cope, possibly nightmares
emotional symptoms:	feeling of not being yourself at times, in bad or low mood most of the time
behaviour:	starting lots of things and not finishing anything

Comments: At this point you are likely to need outside help to get rid of your fear.

LEVEL 8
physical symptoms:	as in level 7, but also likelihood of frequent palpitations, constant tiredness, twitches, nausea
mental symptoms:	feeling out of control, problems thinking rationally
emotional symptoms:	aggressive or oversensitive/tearful a lot of the time, feeling panicky, fear of going crazy
behaviour:	problems communicating without being emotional, irrational, frantic

Comments: This is where the acute state starts. If you are on this level often, you are likely to damage your health unless you take action. Seek professional help.

LEVEL 9

physical symptoms:	as in level 8, but also likelihood of tightness in chest, very shallow breathing, cold sweat, trembling
mental symptoms:	unable to think rationally
emotional symptoms:	severe fits of temper or depression, fits of prolonged crying, feeling that you are crazy
behaviour:	totally erratic, very panicky, no possibility of hiding the panic from onlookers any more

Comments: Seek professional help immediately.

LEVEL 10

physical symptoms:	as in level 9, but also likelihood of 'claw' around the heart, inability to move, feeling rooted to the spot, feeling unable to breathe
mental symptoms:	unable to think
emotional symptoms:	feeling utterly helpless and alone, feeling that you are dying
behaviour:	totally passive or totally freaked out

Comments: Seek professional help immediately.

As you are looking at the 10-Point Fear Scale, you need to bear in mind that every consecutive level will not only contain its own physical, mental and emotional symptoms, but will also contain all the symptoms of all the previous levels.

As suggested earlier, you may want to think about a time recently when your fear was at its worst and see if you can remember any of the symptoms. This will give you a good starting point to try and locate your level on the Fear Scale.

PREMONITION (Level 0–3)

Some of us have a talent to listen to our sixth sense that predicts a future event. We *all* have a sixth sense, but more often than not, we ignore it or rationalize it away because what we perceive subconsciously does not fit in with what we *want* to believe will happen. With the millions of outside stimuli that we are exposed to (or expose ourselves to) every day of the week, our more subtle feelings often get overlooked. The constant bombardment of television, radio, music, newspapers and advertisements, together with a rushed lifestyle, steamroller over the perception of our inner world – we are out of touch with ourselves.

Premonition is *not* the same thing as worrying, even though it might be accompanied by similar physical symptoms. I'm lucky in that one of my sisters, Nada, has occasional premonitions, so her experiences can serve as examples here. Let me give you a few instances.

Nada had always been lucky when it came to competitions or games of chance. Whenever we went to a fun fair as children, Nada more often than not would win something. There was this particular stall where you had to pull a string, choosing out of a bundle of at least 300. At the end of each string was a little bag. Most of the bags had only worthless weights in them, but a few of them had a prize in them. My youngest sister Ljuba and I never won anything; Nada, however, won something most of the time. She would also win competitions in magazines and newspapers and once was sent a bouquet of flowers every two weeks for a whole year as a prize.

One of Nada's premonitions occurred when she and Ljuba were returning home from having visited my father who lives a three-hour-drive away from them. Nada was driving, and they were going down the motorway. The weather was beautiful, with clear blue skies and pleasant warm sunshine, so they decided to leave the motorway and instead continue their way home via a more scenic route along an A road. The road was clear, hardly any traffic, and visibility was excellent as they were whizzing along. Nada likes to drive fast and always does, so when she suddenly started slowing down, Ljuba was taken aback. There was no one in front of them, no one behind them, the road was dry and clear, the landscape openly stretching away with fields and meadows on both sides, and there was absolutely no reason to slow down. Ljuba just looked at Nada without saying anything.

They continued at a slow speed for a little while, and eventually the road went round a curve into a wooded area, and there, on the road, right in front of them, stood a deer. Nada stopped the car easily and the deer started moving to cross the road. Had they continued at the original speed, no doubt they would have had a serious accident.

When Nada and Ljuba talked about this incident as they continued their drive home, Nada explained that as they were driving along the clear stretch of the road she had suddenly had a clear, unequivocal impression that she needed to slow down. It was not like a feeling; it was more like *knowing* something without any doubt in her mind. Driving slowly was the right thing to do, so that was what she did. There was not even the trace of interference from her logical mind – she just accepted a plain fact. At the same time she had no idea *why* she should slow down, and she certainly did not foresee in her mind that there would be a deer standing in the middle of the road as she went around the bend – she was as surprised as Ljuba when she saw the animal.

Looking at the Fear Scale, one would probably have to classify this incident as a Level 0 or 1 since there was no physical reaction to this subconscious message Nada was receiving.

On another occasion, I had decided very spontaneously to surprise Nada with a visit. It was her birthday, which fell on a Saturday. On that Saturday morning, I woke up and decided suddenly to book a flight to go and see her, knowing she had planned a birthday party for later on that day. Two hours later I was at Heathrow, boarding my flight to Frankfurt.

When I arrived at Nada's doorstep, she was delighted to see me, but she also seemed relieved, saying, 'Oh, it's *you* then!' It turned out that all day Saturday, Nada had felt uneasy and a bit perturbed, thinking that someone was coming who hadn't been invited. She racked her brain who it could be but simply couldn't think of anyone. And because the premonition was so strong, she also worried about not having enough crockery for an extra guest, so while I was still in the air on my way to her, she rang Ljuba to ask her to bring an extra set of crockery with her because she expected an uninvited guest. Ljuba arrived a few hours before me because she had promised to help with the preparations for the party, and she confirmed later that Nada kept going on about who that extra person could be . . .

APPREHENSION (Level 1–2)

Being on Level 1 or 2 is ideal for situations like exams or tests, for public speaking or presentations. It is a good state of mind to be in whenever you have to perform in whatever way because it ensures that you are switched on and mentally and physically 'on your toes'.

The difference between premonitions on the one hand and apprehension on the other is that premonitions can sometimes be Level 0, whereas apprehensions will always be at least Level 1. Also, a premonition is always irrational, whereas the feeling of apprehension has a rational basis to it. You are expecting a future event to be difficult or troublesome, and this expectation is often based on previous experience. As a consequence, your body and mind switch into a higher gear to make extra energy available for the increased demands that are to be made on your system*. The physical changes are only slight because no great conflicts are expected. This is the case when you have had overall positive experiences with performance situations so that, even though you are aware that they are more demanding than other everyday tasks, you can still make optimum use of the extra energies provided.

Your expectations are determined by your personality type as well as by relevant experiences in the past. If you are a tidy person and you are expecting a friend to come and stay who you know is very untidy, you may feel apprehensive about her visit. If you are self-assured and know that you will ask her to tidy up, the apprehensive feelings will just function as a warning signal that reminds you that you need to take appropriate action. If, however, you are unable to speak up for yourself or if you have been taught that it is rude to ask guests to conform to

---

When I speak about 'system' in the following, I am referring to the whole person, to the entity of body, mind, emotions and spirit, including all the senses.

certain rules, the likelihood is that the apprehension deteriorates into a Level 3–4 worry.

If someone has proved in the past to be unsympathetic when you tell them about a problem, your consequent apprehension on future occasions will probably caution you not to speak to that person about personal matters again. In this sense, apprehension is very useful because it acts as a protective shield that helps prevent us getting hurt, and it also serves as an instrument for selecting who we trust and who we don't trust. Again, just as with premonitions, we have a tendency to mistrust our own feelings and judgements. Our intellect tells us that we should 'not be so petty' or that we should 'not mind so much' when someone, for example, takes advantage of our readiness to help, when our instincts tell us that this person will only ring when they want something. So we feel apprehensive when we meet that person again.

As opposed to worries, apprehensive feelings are not accompanied by discernible bodily reactions. It is when you notice your body reacting even as you only *think* about the event in question that you have reached the state of worrying.

WORRYING (Level 3–5)

Most people will be quite familiar with this level of fear. If the daily routine is interrupted, if an unusual task lies ahead of you or if you have just found out that you are overdrawn or that a close family member is ill, you will start worrying to a certain extent. If you are the calm type, you may only go up to Level 3, and even if you go higher, you won't stay on the higher level too long. If, however, you are the nervous type, you are much more likely to shoot up to Level 5 straightaway and stay there for quite a long time. Your personal circumstances at the time will further determine how much you are affected.

Consider the following example. You have made a mistake at work which you know is bound to come to your boss's attention the following day. The mistake is embarrassing rather than grave. The possibilities are now as follows:

Your personality	Your boss's personality	Additional circumstances	Probable fear level
calm, good self-esteem	friendly, calm	no other problems	3
calm, good self esteem	nervous, critical	no other problems	4
calm, good self-esteem	friendly, calm	you are over-worked and feel ill	4–5
nervous, self-critical	friendly, calm	no other problems	4–5
nervous, self-critical	nervous, critical	your marriage is about to split up	5
nervous, self-critical	friendly, calm	your marriage is about to split up	5–7
calm, good self-esteem	nervous, critical	you are pregnant and will leave work in a week's time	2–3

There are obviously many more options and possibilities of combinations, but I'm sure you can already see how your level of worrying is influenced by a number of factors.

No doubt there are people who are 'worriers'. They need to have something to worry about, and if there is nothing they will look around until they have found something. It can become a habit, even a way of life, to worry, but it is a habit that has its price. If you worry incessantly on a higher level (Level 5), it means that your body is constantly switched into overdrive.

Even though the level of fear is still manageable at this level, there are physical reactions now which begin to sap your energy. You cannot relax because of all the extra adrenalin that is going around your body without an outlet, so your sleep is affected, and this in turn means you are feeling less refreshed the next morning. Your concentration suffers, you make more mistakes and now you *really* have a reason to worry!

It is a miracle how long the body can stand pressure like that, and even higher pressure, before the strain on our physical resources takes its toll. We can usually get away with living as a worrier for quite a number of years, but eventually the immune system is weakened and we are much more likely to catch colds, the flu or a stomach bug; we are much more likely to develop stomach ulcers or headaches. Most of these problems are not serious, but as we have seen in the table above, if circumstances change unfavourably, this can push us even higher up on the fear scale, and this can result in problems like phobias or anxiety which are much more difficult to deal with.

It is often thought that it is a sign of 'caring' if you are worried about someone else. An old myth has it that unless you worry over your husband or children, you are not a good wife and mother. Unless you make a fuss over your family, pressing unwilling children into warm anoraks, forcing extra food on them and interfering in all sorts of other aspects of their lives, you feel you are not doing your job as a mother properly. It is almost like a superstition that unless you worry, the disasters you are worrying about are going to happen.

If you feel you are a worrier, it may be of great help if you start working on this problem. You will see that not only will you feel better for it, but also all those around you will be relieved!

PHOBIAS (Level 5–9)

A phobia is an excessive, unrealistic, uncontrollable fear which is triggered off by a particular object, activity or situation. The word 'phobia' comes from the Greek and means 'panic fear'.

A phobia is characterized by three factors which distinguish it from ordinary fears. Firstly, the feeling of fear is *persistent* over a long period of time. Secondly, the fear is *unreasonable*, and even though you can see that clearly, this recognition does not help you get rid of the phobia. Thirdly, having a phobia always entails you endeavouring to *avoid* the feared object, activity or situation.

There are three different types of phobias. There are *simple phobias* where the fear is directed towards one specific object or situation. You can be phobic about birds, spiders, worms, moths, thunder or water for example, and you can also be phobic about being trapped and therefore avoid lifts. In all of these instances, the person experiencing the phobia is afraid of being killed or injured if they allow the object of their phobia to get close to them.

Simple phobias can often be traced back to specific traumatic experiences. One of my clients, a 33-year-old secretary, had a phobia about getting her head wet which caused her considerable problems when she went to the hairdressers. She was OK as long as she could lean forward to have her hair washed, but she would immediately panic if she lay back to do so. We eventually discovered that, as a very young child, she had fallen backwards off a wall into a puddle and had had quite a shock. Ever since then her panic was linked with getting her head wet from behind.

Another type of phobia is *social phobia*. The fear here is that of embarrassing yourself in front of other people. People with a social phobia will therefore avoid urinating in public toilets, will shun parties and conferences, and refuse to eat in restaurants and cafes, and so on.

Social phobias can also go back to a traumatic event in the past, with the phobic situation in the present being an emotional 'translation' of the original embarrassing event. One of my clients had a phobia of eating in restaurants and could only be persuaded to do so if it was late in the evening and the restaurant was only dimly lit so that others could not see him too well. His phobia went back 30 years to an incident at school where he had been humiliated in front of friends – in the school dining hall.

The third type of phobia is the *fear of panic attacks* and therefore the avoidance of situations where you cannot easily escape unobserved, for example queues in the supermarket, theatres and cinemas, bridges, buses, trains and all forms of public transport. As this condition is more complex than the other two forms of phobia, I have dedicated a separate section to it (see pp. 60–1).

A phobia constitutes a very strong physical reaction to a particular stimulus, with highly negative mental and behavioural side effects. If the object of the phobia is one that can be avoided easily, the sufferer may lead a comparatively normal life. Snakes, for example, are not very common in England, and certainly not in big cities, so the only thing the phobic person will have to avoid is the reptile section of their local zoo.

However, if the phobia is particularly strong, this person may also avoid walking barefoot on the grass in their garden or avoid going for walks through meadows or walking through forests with a lot of undergrowth, and this would obviously infringe on their life much more.

As phobics try and avoid the object or situation that they are afraid of, the fear becomes even more pronounced. As the fear is not faced and therefore never checked against reality, it becomes a thing in itself and grows out of all proportion in the sufferer's mind. It is a vicious circle where you avoid something because you are afraid of it, so you grow even more afraid and consequently avoid it even more rigorously. You end up trapping yourself in your own fear.

AGORAPHOBIA AND PANIC ATTACKS
(Level 6–10)

The severity of agoraphobia can fluctuate between levels 6 and 10, whereas a panic attack is always a level 10. Levels 8 and 9 constitute extremely high degrees of anxiety, whereas a level 10 is the explosion of accumulated anxiety.

The term agoraphobia was first used towards the end of the nineteenth century. The word agoraphobia is derived from the Greek *agora* meaning 'market place' and phobia meaning 'panic fear', and originally denoted a condition where a person is unable to walk out into open and public spaces such as streets or squares, or, if they do, they experience severe anxiety. Nowadays, the term encompasses a wider range of symptoms, including situations where a person suffers a high level of fear when they are away from the safety of their own home, and in particular when they are in crowded or isolated places where escape is impossible or help not available.

Agoraphobics establish a mental radius around their home within which they can just about manage to operate, but past which they would never dream of venturing. In some cases, this radius becomes so small that people cannot even walk out of their own front door, and in severe cases, agoraphobics can even become afraid of being on their own at home.

In contrast to the simple phobias, agoraphobia is not a fear of a particular object or situation, but rather a fear of a panic attack arising when they are away from help in an isolated place, or when they are in a crowded place where it is difficult to escape. Agoraphobics will therefore typically avoid bridges ('If I have a panic attack when I'm in the middle I won't make it to the other side where someone can help me!') and will certainly never sit in the middle of a row in a cinema or theatre ('If a panic attack hits me suddenly I'll freak out and won't be able to get out quickly, and all these people will think I'm totally mad.')

The main fear about a possible panic attack is that you could faint or have a heart attack, or that you could lose control and make a fool of yourself. Many agoraphobics are also claustrophobic (fearing enclosed spaces such as lifts), and they are also afraid of heights and flying, for all the aforementioned reasons.

Just like people suffering from simple phobias and social phobias, agoraphobics are trying to control their symptoms by avoiding those situations that might bring on a panic attack. Unfortunately, this avoidance perpetuates the fear and allows it to become worse, and that ultimately results in a continuous narrowing of the mobility radius. There are people with agoraphobia who haven't left their home in years!

Before agoraphobia develops, there are usually one or two isolated incidents of panic attacks, often in an emotionally stressful situation. Frequently, there is an interval of one year to several years between these one-off attacks, and they do not necessarily always lead to full blown agoraphobia later. Depending on circumstances, they can remain one-off occurrences, but more often than not they don't.

Agoraphobia is a condition that severely restricts your daily life and has a negative effect on your social life (and often also puts strain on your marriage and home life). It is estimated that between 70 and 80 per cent of sufferers are female.

ANXIETY (Level 6–9)

The word anxiety is derived from the Latin *anxius*, meaning agitation and distress. Anxiety denotes a persistent state of fear which can be distinguished from other types of fear such as phobias because it is not directed towards anything concrete. It is quite understandable if you are afraid of not being able to meet a deadline at work or of being late for an important meeting or of failing an exam, but when you are anxious, you are afraid of anything and everything.

Someone suffering from anxiety might have a diffuse feeling of impending disaster or a vague but persistent fear of what is going to happen in the future. Because this type of fear is not connected with any particular situation, it is also called *free floating anxiety*.

Even though anxiety levels will fluctuate during the day and will be worse on some days than on others, it is always there in the back of the person's mind. There may even be hours where the person feels free of anxiety, and in these rare moments it is as if a heavy burden has been lifted off their shoulders, but these moments of reprieve do not last, and soon the agitated feelings return.

Because the sufferer cannot make out *why* they are agitated, they often feel that they must be going mad. Their anxiety accompanies them everywhere they go. They can be with good friends who they have known for years and still have a feeling of agitation and discomfort. They can do something that they used to enjoy doing, like watching a beautiful sunset, and still be unable to relax and appreciate it because they feel nervous and on edge.

As a consequence, anxiety sufferers often behave in an excessively timid and fearful way, or they appear to be moody. This will often cause concern with family and friends who are quite willing to help but cannot do so because the sufferer cannot give them a reason for their symptom. This is why sufferers are often told that they should just try a bit harder to 'pull themselves together' or 'not to be silly'. (This is obviously not a very helpful remark to make — surely the suffer him- or herself is quite fed up with the symptoms and would gladly pull themselves together if only they could!)

Anxiety can also show itself as aggressive behaviour which is an unfortunate attempt at bulldozing over the agitation. Being aggressive is a bit like producing a release of tension in order to gain relief from the anxiety, similar to the release that a panic attack achieves spontaneously.

Enduring and handling those constant feelings of inner

agitation is very tiring. Because your system is continuously working on overload, you end up physically and mentally exhausted and depressed. That makes you want to withdraw and pull away from anything that could produce stress. Any upsets in your daily routine become a disaster because all your strength is needed to keep your anxiety at bay, so no strength is available to deal with adapting to changes. When you suffer from high level anxiety, it is as if you have become allergic to life.

When anxiety has reached this stage, it can no longer be considered a mere warning signal — it has now become a force in itself which controls the sufferer's life. Having to endure chronic anxiety is as crippling as any physical disability.

When we look more closely at what is behind this apparently motiveless fear, and when we talk to sufferers at length, we invariably find that there *is* a motive for their fear, that this fear has been evoked through one or several real events that triggered off a negative chain of thoughts which then made the original fear spiral into more severe anxiety.

OBSESSIVE-COMPULSIVE DISORDERS
(Level 7–9)

We speak of an *obsession* when a person has a persistent idea or desire in their mind which they can perceive as being irrational but which they cannot stop themselves from thinking about. The obsessive person usually despises these thoughts and rejects them intellectually but still cannot escape them. In order to counteract these terrifying thoughts, the obsessive person will often go through a ritualistic *compulsive* action. A thought or a habit is only considered an obsession or a compulsion if the person concerned cannot stop it or if they waste a great deal of time carrying out the compulsive actions so that it disrupts their everyday life.

There are a great number of different obsessions and compulsions. You can have a mild obsession where you give a special significance to certain colours or where you try to avoid certain numbers because they are 'unlucky'. In this mild form, one would most commonly classify them as superstitions that are based on folklore. However, if someone goes to great lengths to avoid certain colours or numbers, these thoughts have obviously become obsessive.

Other obsessions are those of a sexual nature, involving thoughts of incest or homosexuality, and there are also obsessions with exactness and symmetry where everything has to be in a particular order. Other examples of obsessions are exaggerated concern with dirt and germs or body wastes or secretion. Obsessions of a more severe nature involve thoughts of violence, fear of harming others or oneself, fear of blurting out obscenities or fear of being held responsible for something going wrong.

Common compulsions are those of counting over and over again to a certain number; checking and rechecking doors, windows, locks or taps; repeatedly ordering and arranging items; hoarding and collecting items such as newspapers or mail. Again, just like with obsessions, the level of anxiety depends on how much these compulsions distress the person concerned and how much time they occupy. You may insist on hanging the toilet roll with the end facing the wall, and whenever you find it the 'wrong' way around, you may want to change it to the 'right' way around. Even though this has the trait of compulsion, it would generally not be termed such — one would be much more likely to call it fussiness. This, however, is not the level that we are concerned with here since this behaviour is not accompanied by feelings of fear or anxiety.

However, when a person feels incapable of resisting their obsessive thoughts or compulsive rituals, the anxiety level can go all the way up to a Level 9. At this point, the person needs a lot of help from others because he or she simply cannot function normally on their own.

It has been found that it is a certain personality type who is potentially prone to developing an obsessive-compulsive disorder. (*However, please note that you will not necessarily develop an obsessive-compulsive disorder just because you have one or all of the following characteristics!*) This personality type is someone who finds it difficult to express positive and warm emotions, is highly critical of themselves and others, a perfectionist who will always put work before pleasure. This person will furthermore be unwilling or unable to make decisions for fear of making the wrong decision, and they will be overconscientious and inflexible. They are virtually locked into an inner and outer prison by their personality and by the resulting obsessive and compulsive problem.

Sufferers feel helpless in view of their problems and ashamed that they cannot manage to control themselves, and this sometimes prevents them from seeking help for years. It is often only when they find they simply cannot function any more that they are persuaded by family or friends to embark on some form of therapy to alleviate the symptoms.

Both hypno-analysis and behaviour therapy have proved successful in treating these problems. Very good results have also been achieved with paradoxical intention (see p. 131 ff) and gradual desensitization (see p. 106 ff), and follow-ups suggest that these positive results are lasting.

DIFFERENT CATEGORIES

Having looked at the different levels, let us have a look at the various classifications that we can group fears under.

Any of the following categories can occur at any of the aforementioned levels, depending on your personality, the severity of the fear-inducing situation, your personal circumstances at the time and other people's reactions to you and your fear problem.

Ways of solving these fear problems are either included in the following chapters or can be found in the second part of the book.

FEAR OF FAILURE

This fear category contains situations in which you have to demonstrate a particular skill or knowledge on an *official* basis. This includes exams and tests, going to job interviews, public speaking and also male sexual performance, amongst others. In all these cases, you are aware that you have a high visibility factor and that others will assess you on your performance, benevolently or otherwise. And it's the 'otherwise' that gets you worrying!

Fear of failure is a mixture of worrying and phobia. It is like a greatly magnified bout of worry about a particular situation. The only thing that distinguishes it from a phobia is that the dreaded situation is generally considered to be genuinely difficult (with the exception of male sexual performance), whereas with a phobia, the fear is always unreasonable.

Anyone would agree that having to sit an exam or take a test could make you apprehensive or even nervous. Some people are affected more than others by such a situation, but everyone is affected to some extent. It is generally acknowledged that exam situations put pressure on you and can therefore create tension.

The same is true for public speaking, particularly for those who don't speak in front of an audience on a regular basis. To put yourself voluntarily into a position where you become the centre of attention and consequently vulnerable to criticism can create great anxiety. So when a friend confesses to being nervous about a presentation they have to give at work the next day, we can sympathize with them because we know we would probably feel the same in a similar situation.

Male sexual performance is another area where awareness of being assessed can have a devastating effect on your ability to perform. The tricky thing is that an erection depends on you concentrating on certain arousing thought patterns, and these thought patterns cannot unfold unless you are relaxed. So if you fail on one occasion to have a satisfactory erection or to maintain the erection long enough for intercourse to take place, there is a possibility of anticipatory fear the next time, and this makes another failure more likely.

Fear of exams, fear of public speaking and fear of sexual incompetence all have one thing in common – the person is perfectly capable of performing as long as nobody else is present. The student who flunks his exam has revised diligently and knows all the answers in class. The young woman who fails her driving test did a beautiful three-point-turn only the day before. The employee who gets flustered when giving a presentation to colleagues is an expert in his subject and spoke fluently when he rehearsed at home. The man who has problems in bed with his partner is perfectly capable of having satisfactory erections and ejaculations when he is by himself.

In order to perform well, you need to be wholly absorbed in what you are doing, to an extent where you almost have tunnel vision so that it becomes irrelevant where you are at the time and who is watching.

One of my clients had an extraordinary ability to do just that. Even though she was extremely nervous to the degree of panic before every exam, she could switch over and be totally calm and concentrated the minute she sat down and turned over the test paper. She would work through the questions quickly and competently so that she always finished before anyone else. She even had time to check through her answers at the end. She always passed all her exams, despite her panic the day before, simply because she had the ability to get so wrapped up in what she was doing that she 'forgot' that it was an exam.

Fear of failure usually coincides with a lack of confidence and often with a general feeling of not being in control of your life, and this in turn can occur in conjunction with general anxiety.

Fear of failure can have various causes. When there is a lot of pressure on a child to perform well all the time, when failure to excel is frowned upon, an over-emphasis is placed on academic or sports achievements, often at the expense of other values. A child who is, however subtly, given to understand that his or her popularity with their parents depends on how well he or she performs at school, is more likely to develop a fear of failure than a child who gets unconditional love, no matter how well or badly they are doing at school.

When parental pressure in childhood has been particularly strong and nothing was ever good enough, a person can either become a workaholic in later life, still striving to attain perfection to appease their parents (even if they have long since died), or that person can simply give up and withdraw into a job that is well beneath their capabilities because they feel unable to or refuse to strive for perfection any longer. They become afraid of success because once they are successful, they would have to worry that they could not keep up this high level of achievement.

In other cases, the damage is done at school by teachers who react with disdain and punishment towards children who don't do well or cannot answer questions. In my hypnotherapy practice I have found many instances where fear of failure goes back to one or several traumatic events at school where a teacher ridiculed and humiliated a child in front of the whole class.

With sexual problems, the cause can also go back into the early years of your life. When premature ejaculation or impotence have always been a problem, it stands to reason that the cause lies way back in time *before* the person failed for the first time. Excessively strict moral upbringing or a domineering and humiliating mother can make the son feel helpless and emasculated, and this can then all too easily lead to sexual problems.

If, however, the sexual problem started when a particular partner came onto the scene, chances are that something is wrong with the relationship and the man picks up the negative vibes. As sexual arousal, erection and ejaculation are dependent on very finely balanced mental processes, a lack of trust or fear of being criticized by the partner can result in a loss of spontaneity and therefore impotence. The problem is often spontaneously overcome with a new partner.

I must emphasize in this context that most instances of impotence are only temporary. Being overworked, stressed or overtired can result in impotence for that particular day, but on the whole, the problem rights itself as soon as the man has recovered his physical strength.

FEAR OF SEPARATION

When I think about fear of separation, the first image that springs to mind is that of a small child crying and clinging to its mother when she is about to leave it at the playschool for the first time.

Not all children are the same of course. Some children are bolder than others and can be left in kindergarten relatively easily. However, one has to bear in mind that separation is a serious matter for children, especially little children who experience being away from home without their mother or father for the first time.

A child's reaction to this new experience will depend not

only on the child's personality, but also on how safe that child feels with its parents generally.

Panic strikes easily with little children when they find themselves in a strange place. Because the environment is new and all the people in the new environment are unfamiliar, they can get frightened quite easily. (This fear is also known in adults. Remember when you started a new job and how worried you were about the fact that you did not know anybody there?)

To a child, separation is an *existential* issue. Put yourself into a child's shoes as it goes along to its first day at playschool: there you are, amongst strange adults and children, in a strange place, and your mum tells you that you should stay here for a while and that she will come and pick you up very soon, and then she walks away from you and waves just the way you do when grandma and grandpa leave after their visit to your house – and then the grandparents don't come back for ages!

It is important, particularly if a child is of an anxious disposition, to take some time to ease him or her into an unfamiliar situation, for example by taking him to the kindergarten or playschool a few times, showing him around and explaining things, without leaving him there.

Sometimes children can be made to feel overanxious if parents are particularly strict or cautious themselves (see also p. 10 about copying fear). If children are heavily restricted from expressing themselves or punished for exploring, they can lose confidence in themselves. As a consequence, they feel inadequate and that makes them more dependent on one of their parents being with them all the time.

But it is not just children who suffer from fear of separation in a family. Parents can also feel it is a struggle to let children go. Just as children are dependent on their parents, so parents grow to become dependent on their children.

As children come along within a relationship, the parents have to learn to cope with their changed family situation and the problems that arise through each new arrival. The pleasures of child rearing are often balanced by stresses and frustrations that arise, especially for the person who is closest to the children, which nowadays is still mainly the mother. After having worked and earned her own money and lived as an adult, the mother now goes back to live in a world of children.

In contrast, the father still has his work and, through his work, contact with adults, so that he is able to enjoy the children as an added dimension to his life.

When children are beginning to move out, parents usually go through a crisis. As the children leave the parental home, a new era begins. The children are now adult, making their own independent choices and decisions and possibly starting their own families. For the parents, a change occurs too — they are making the transition from parents to grandparents, a landmark that they are now beginning to approach old age. Moreover, the parents' lives now have to focus again on one another. If by this stage the marriage has grown apart and communication between the partners has been conducted mainly via the children, the fact that the children are no longer available as a buffer zone within a deteriorated marriage can cause anxiety.

It is at this point that some mothers begin to cling to their children. By keeping the children attached to them, the mother's focus is averted from the unpleasant prospect of having to face the rest of her life with her husband in a relationship that is no longer satisfactory.

If it is difficult for a married couple to let go of their children, it is even more difficult for single parents. As there is no partner, the child or children constitute the main point of attention in the parent's life. Where in a two-parent family, childrearing can be divided (however unequally) between two people, a single parent has a much more intense one-to-one relationship with their child or children. A mother in a two-parent family may go to work *despite* the children; a single mother will go to work *for* the children. This particular closeness between mother and child can make it particularly difficult to allow the child to leave.

Eventually, most families manage to find a balance between allowing the children to separate from the parents and yet remain involved with them on a new, adult basis.

Fear of separation can also play a role in adult relationships, often with very negative results. Being in a relationship is habit forming, just as being on your own is. When you have been in a relationship for a while, you get used to having someone else there. Being with another person on an everyday basis becomes somewhat addictive for many people, even though the relationship may not be very good.

The longer the relationship goes on, the harder it can become to contemplate going it alone again. There is a certain comfort in having someone else there, however unsatisfactory this person may be. Often it is only when the situation becomes unbearable to the extreme that people can overcome their fear of separation and take positive action.

The key to a solution in these relationship dependencies lies in considering the long-term goals you have for your life. If you find it difficult to leave a detrimental relationship, think about the consequences of remaining in your present situation. If you can honestly say that you have done your best to sort out any differences and have worked on improving the relationship to the best of your ability *and it is still not working*, chances are that it never will. If you still stay, you are blocking your own way to ever achieving a satisfactory relationship with someone else.

If, on the other hand, you are serious about wanting to find a partner who is truly compatible with you, you need to leave your present one to make it possible for the right person to be with you. Yes, your life will be different without your old partner; yes, you may find it difficult initially to make the transition from partnership to single life, but it does become easier. If you lack the confidence to take that final step, look at the section on solutions for ways of overcoming your fear.

FEAR OF LOSS

I am writing this book in 1992 while Great Britain is going through very difficult times indeed. With a continuously depressed economy, thousands of people have already lost their jobs and many more will lose theirs over the next few months.

The spectre that stalks so many households today is the fear that the main breadwinner might lose his or her job. Every time you look in the papers or watch the news on television, there are new reports of redundancies, bankruptcies and closures, and many employees are aware (even though it might not have been officially announced) that their company is in dire financial straits.

This fear of redundancy is made worse by the fact that, as an employee, you generally don't have access to accurate information about the status quo of your company – your fear is usually based on what you hear through the grapevine. Management are reluctant to enlighten the workforce lest their morale and productivity should deteriorate, and employees get stressed with the uncertainty of their situation.

Losing your job is a traumatic event at the best of times. It knocks your confidence, often quite severely, and it totally changes your life and your routines unless you are able to find another job fairly quickly, and this is less likely while the economy is still in recession.

The disaster of losing your job does not stop there though. As there is no money coming in, people find it hard to keep up payments for their mortgage, so that they could also lose the family home in the process. In extreme cases where whole branches of industry are closed down, whole communities can be wiped out.

These are bleak prospects if you are working for a company that is going downhill, and a fear of loss is only too understandable. When you are worried about losing your job, it is doubly important to control your stress. There is nothing you can do if your company makes you redundant, but at least you can make sure that your health does not suffer through stress-related illness. Make a point of keeping to a healthy diet, exercise, think positively to keep your spirits up, look for other job opportunities, look into alternatives, *be active*. If you allow your fear to defeat you, you are truly defeated.

Another situation where the fear of loss can arise is that of seeing a person close to you gradually die of a fatal disease like AIDS or some forms of cancer. Just as the dying person is going through various emotional stages, so are the people who are closest to them.

It puts enormous stress on you when you have to watch your partner or your child fade away, often in discomfort and pain. The pain and fear of losing that person is often mingled with a feeling of guilt. You feel that you have no right to your pain and fear because *they* are the ones who are going through pain and despair, *they* are the ones who are going through the frightening process of dying.

It is an experience that requires enormous strength to see a loved one through to the end, and your pain and fear deserves as much attention as that of the dying person. Make sure you get support, either from other family members, from friends or from a professional counsellor. Don't carry your fears all by yourself; enlist help and talk it through to make the burden more bearable.

The same advice goes for anyone who finds themselves in a situation where they have to have an operation that results in the removal of a part of the body. In many cases, cancer can only be eradicated by removing a large area of tissue around the affected area, and in the chest area, this can mean for some women that one of the breasts has to be removed. In other cases, a leg has to be amputated, either after an accident or through circulatory problems caused by smoking; or large parts of the bowels have to be removed and the person will have to carry an *anus praeter* where they discharge their stool into a bag that is fitted to an artificial outlet on the belly.

Coming up to any of these operations is extremely traumatic because you know you will be losing a part of your body. It is a difficult choice to make – in order to save your life you need to permit your doctor to cripple your body.

It is now widely recognized that people in situations similar to the above need psychological support after the operation, but it is still sometimes overlooked that the same support is necessary in the time leading up to the operation. If you are awaiting surgery of that kind, do seek professional help with your fears. There are a number of organizations and charities which will be experienced in helping people who are facing your particular problem. Please use them, that's what they are there for.

A very different fear of loss is the feeling of jealousy. Here, the fear of loss is not so much paired with sadness but with anger. A jealous person is someone who lives in fear that their partner will find someone else more attractive and leave them for that other person.

It can sometimes be quite difficult to determine whether there is a foundation to this feeling of jealousy. If your partner flirts with others but is cold towards you, you may feel you have good reason for jealousy. If your partner has a history of infidelity, your suspicions may be equally justified. If, however, you do not find any obvious signs that something is going on behind your back, or if you have always been jealous with every partner you have had, chances are that the problem lies with you rather than with your partner.

If your partner gives you real reasons to feel jealous, you will need to sort things out with him or her. You will have to talk about your feelings and explain what it is he or she does that makes you feel uncomfortable (see also Vera Peiffer, *Positive Thinking*). If the relationship is fundamentally good, your partner will take notice of what you say and do his or her best to change behaviour that makes you feel anxious and angry. If, however, your partner doesn't make any efforts to alleviate the problem, you are in the wrong relationship and will have to get out (see also Vera Peiffer, *How To Cope With Splitting Up*).

When your partner is not giving you grounds for jealousy but you still feel that fear of loss, mingled with anger, you may find it useful to think about yourself. How confident are you in yourself? How much does your positive self-image depend on your partner? Do you feel like a nobody without your partner? When you see your partner as a means of propping up your ego, then of course it becomes desperately important that your partner should be available and present all the time. If you are very insecure about your own worth, you may be using your partner to feed your flagging self-esteem by him or her giving you constant attention.

All this has nothing to do with love. Jealousy of that kind is an ultimately destructive act of possessiveness which is born out of an inability to value and love yourself. Jealousy ultimately destroys a relationship by suffocating it. As you try and monitor your partner's every move and openly doubt his or her honesty towards you, you are pushing them more and more into a corner. First, they will try and convince you that you have no grounds to be suspicious, but explanations and reassurances like that usually go into a bottomless pit with a jealous person. Because jealous people need *constant* reassurance, they will never be satisfied, and the partner gets more and more frustrated with the futility of their attempts to reassure.

Sadly, the jealous person brings about what they fear most — the loss of their partner.

If you feel you have a jealousy problem, don't despair — help is available. Read through the section on hypno-analysis on pp. 137–47. A lack of confidence and self-esteem can be sorted out so that you can continue through life a happier person who can enjoy a good relationship.

FEAR OF THE FUTURE

None of us know what the future holds, and yet some of us spend a lot of time worrying about it. We read about the damage that is being done to our environment, the deplorable state of our rivers, forests and seas; the decimation of certain types of animals, with some species already extinct; political upheaval in so many parts of the world and the poverty and misery of the homeless and refugees here and elsewhere. Not exactly a reason to rejoice!

It can be very depressing to open a newspaper these days. Where is it all going to end? Do we have a future at all, or will it all end in disaster?

Some people feel so negative about the state of the world that they have decided not to bring any children into it. Others go as far as spending their lives in preparation for THE END which they say is imminent. Extreme cases, admittedly, but they do exist. Most of us will be far removed from these extremes, but we are certainly aware and often worried about what is going on around us and where it might lead in the future.

Human nature is such that we are only frightened if something happens so close to our front door that we can't possibly overlook it any more. If we live near a nuclear power station and we hear about a leak there, we get very worried and try to find out what happened and whether we are in any danger. If we read about a leak at a *foreign* nuclear reactor, however, we turn to the TV page to see what's on telly that evening . . .

This is the average reaction of the majority of people. We are only concerned about a war somewhere far away if it could have repercussions on us directly.

People who are excessively frightened by what the future of the world might hold tend to be people who suffer from anxiety in their private life. Often, the pessimism they project into the future derives from anxiety problems rooted in their present (see also section on anxiety, pp. 61–3). The less you feel in control of your own life, the more alarming the future looks. The fear within yourself translates into everything you see outside yourself – other people become scary because they are more confident or different from you, and negative events that happen around you deepen your feelings of hopelessness and despair even further. The worst thing about all this is that your negative premonitions are based on facts – you have seen it in black and white in all the newspapers. They have proved to you that the future looks grim! These reports only reinforce your own depression, and this makes you look at life in an even more negative way.

Lots of people read these alarming news reports, but not all of them get frightened. Those people who deal with the negative information in a constructive way start doing their share in helping, for example, the environment. They re-use their carrier bags, they recycle paper and glass, they don't buy fur coats and they support a charity of their choice. In other words, they do what they can to help preserve the future of this planet. There may be lots of things we cannot change in life, but there are an awful lot of things we *can* improve.

You may think that this is a drop in the ocean, but think again. Have you noticed how all these movements have gathered momentum? There are containers for glass and paper everywhere nowadays (unheard of ten years ago); manufacturers have actually changed their products to avoid releasing CFC gases (initially, the campaigners for the protection of the ozone layer were considered freaks); Harrods had to close their fur department within five years of the Lynx campaign to abolish the fur trade; Greenpeace and Amnesty now have influence with governments and are continuing to help better the state of the world.

These are just a few examples – there are hundreds more. These positive developments are just as much reality as the negative ones, but unfortunately, bad news sells more newspapers, so that is why we don't seem to hear too much about positive events which could give us a less negative view of our future.

If you are worried about the future, please do something about it. Turn your worry into constructive action and participate in the solution. If you are someone suffering from anxiety and your anxiety makes you despair about the future, please do something about your anxiety. We need you and your input to keep the constructive work going, work that is already happening everywhere around us to solve the problems on our planet.

PART TWO

The Solutions

3. Freedom from Fear

By now, you will have acquainted yourself with the various degrees and categories of fears, and you will also have a fair idea of where your own particular fear fits into the system as outlined in Part 1 of the book.

In the following section, I will ask you to be even more specific about defining your particular fear. In order to help you with this task, I have devised a table that will enable you to monitor your fear on a day-to-day basis. Monitoring is important because it will help you determine which approach, or combination of approaches, you need to take to overcome your problem. You can achieve very good results with self-help techniques in many cases, but at the same time, there are instances in the level 7–10 categories where outside help is needed, either through group or individual therapy.

Before you can make any decisions in that respect, you need to establish your status quo. You need to monitor the frequency with which your fear occurs, the intensity on a physical and behavioural level, and how long each episode of fear lasts. As a rule of thumb you can say that the greater the frequency and the more intense the physical and emotional repercussions of each incident are, the more likely it is that you will need outside help. In the following sections, I have marked clearly where I consider the method suitable for self-help and where the method can only be applied by an expert, such as a psychologist, a behaviourist, a hypnotherapist or other professionals. In this context, I have decided to assign *support groups* to the 'self-help' category because I understand them to be a gathering of people who suffer from similar problems and who help one another by talking openly about the problems they are experiencing and look for solutions by swapping ideas and giving each other moral support. These groups are often chaired by people who have overcome their particular fear problem and are in a position to give very sound advice. In contrast, whenever a professionally trained person is present who supervises the group by setting tasks and helping participants work through the problem, I will use the term *group therapy*, which will bring this approach into the 'therapy' bracket.

In the next section, you will be asked to start a diary and keep it for two or three months. This will not only provide you with a clearer insight into your own situation, but it will also be very useful to take along to a therapist should it turn out you need to see one. Your notes will give him or her valuable information and thus speed up the fact-finding process.

Should you still be unsure about whether to go for a self-help programme or for professional help, you can also use the following sections by working through the self-help steps first and see how far they get you. You may find that applying the self-help strategies enables you to control your fear to a degree where it becomes manageable, even though it has not gone altogether. When you feel that you do not have the time or the money to see a therapist at that particular point in time, you may find that a partial solution is better than no solution at all, and you can always go and see a therapist later. You may, on the other hand, find that the self-help programme is all you need to resolve your fear.

But now, let us have a look at your initial diary.

ESTABLISHING THE STATUS QUO
Self-help
For all types of fear

When we were talking about the 10-Point Fear Scale (pp. 49–52), I had already asked you to establish what the highest level of fear is that you have experienced so far in connection with your particular problem. If you found it difficult to determine your level, keeping a diary will help pinpoint the symptoms that accompany your feeling of fear so that you can then refer back to the 10-Point Fear Scale.

The table has been divided up into sections that are similar to the 10-Point Fear Scale, but I have added a few additional items which are important. The blank outline of the diary is on page 84. Let us go through the various sections.

Fear Level
morning/afternoon/evening

In this section, you should enter the fear level that you experienced at that particular time of day, using the 1–10 scale as outlined on pp. 49–52. If your fear level fluctuates, jot down the highest point of fluctuation, in other words, if you felt very bad on waking up and you would rate this experience as a level 8, and the fear slowly subsided towards lunch time to a level 6, then please mark down the 8 under 'morning'. Equally, if you have an up and down time that oscillates between levels 3 and 5, write down the 5.

As a rule of thumb you can say that if you have levels 7–10 in this section every third day or even more often, you might need professional help in order to solve your problem.

At this point, I would like to emphasize again that any grading of your fear level is by necessity subjective, and this is perfectly all right. You are not establishing a scientific chart here but monitoring your own feelings.

Events

Note down anything unusual that happened during the day. Unforeseen events can heighten your stress level and thus exacerbate the feelings of fear. Events that could come under this category are, for example, getting a letter from the bank, having problems at work, an argument with your children or spouse, having to speak at a meeting the next day, or even expecting friends or in-laws for a visit. Your entries in this section will highlight whether your fear is a specific one, for example a social phobia, or whether it is a more generalized anxiety which makes you afraid of everything and everyone.

A typical pattern for a specific phobia would be that, on average, the general fear level is low, somewhere between 3 and

Day	Fear level morn/aft/evg	Events	Physical symptoms	Mental/ emotional symptoms	Coping strategies	Sleep	Period
MON	morn aft evg						
TUE	morn aft evg						
WED	morn aft evg						
THU	morn aft evg						
FRI	morn aft evg						
SAT	morn aft evg						
SUN	morn aft evg						

4 perhaps, and only when the phobic situation arises will the level go up to 7 or 8. With a specific phobia, you can also observe how the *anticipation* of encountering the phobic situation results in a heightened level of fear — just *thinking* about having to have an injection in a week's time can get the level up to a high mark. With phobias, the relationship between 'Fear Level' and 'Events' is quite clear cut; you can see how they are directly interrelated.

The anxiety pattern, however, is less logically related when you look at the level of fear and the events section. You can have an above average fear level, say 6 or 7, without having anything particular in the events section. Anxiety can even arise when all the circumstances are favourable, when there is no pressure at all, like for example on holiday where you would expect to be able to relax and thereby bring down the stress level.

Physical symptoms

Don't bother writing down every last detail here. It is sufficient if you just mark down the main symptoms. Use abbreviations such as hd (headaches), diz (dizziness), st (stomach) and so on to fit it into the space, and maybe write down somewhere which letters stand for which symptom so you can use them consistently. Also include here if you are overeating or unable to eat as a result of your fear. Use the table on p. 39 as reference.

Mental/emotional symptoms

As under 'physical symptoms', use abbreviations for conditions such as d (depression), con (lack of concentration), f (fidgeting), dis (feelings of dissociation) etc. Use the table on p. 42 as reference.

Coping Strategies

Begin to monitor how you deal with your fear. If you experience anything from level 5 upwards, check what it is you are automatically doing to lessen the impact of your fear. There are a number of possible ways of doing that. Here are some of them:

- drinking alcohol
- taking tablets
- taking exercise
- thinking a lot about the problem
- getting out of the house
- withdrawing (going to bed early; not answering the phone)
- making excuses to avoid a potentially fear-inducing situation
- distracting your attention (knitting; watching TV; reading)
- switching off and pretending the fear-inducing situation doesn't exist
- working a lot
- drifting off into a daydream
- ringing a friend and talking about it

Not all of the above coping strategies are constructive, on the contrary. Some of them are unhelpful because they add an additional problem to the original one. Drinking, taking tablets or drugs and other avoidance behaviours give power to the fear *and* add the complications of addiction. Other strategies are more productive, for example taking exercise or talking about the fear.

This section is important, especially if you have a positive way of dealing with your fear, because you can then expand on this strategy (see also the section on positive thinking, pp. 122–31). Should you find that you are employing negative strategies, then it is still useful to have discovered and acknowledged their existence. As you get better with the help of new and more productive methods, you can begin gradually to abandon the old unconstructive ways.

Sleep

As we have seen in Part 1 of the book, fear can be caused through exhaustion, and one of the side effects of physical and emotional burn-out is the inability to sleep. Sleeping problems can either manifest themselves as an inability to fall asleep, or a tendency to wake up during the night, resulting in a disrupted sleep pattern. Or you may find that you wake up hours before the appropriate time and are unable to go back to sleep. Sometimes all three of these symptoms can occur.

Insomnia wears you out, and it feeds on your nerves if it goes on over a prolonged period of time. If you wake up most mornings and feel tired, you soon exhaust your physical resources. Sleeping is the body's way of recharging the batteries, and if this recharging does not take place on a regular basis, you begin to run on empty during the day, and this can easily produce feelings of fear.

The system also works the other way round of course. Because you are afraid during the day, you may find it difficult to sleep, and this in turn leads to an aggravation of your problem – because you are afraid, you cannot sleep, so you get very tired, and that makes the fear worse, and so on.

As you are observing your sleep pattern, also look at your activities late at night. Are you drinking coffee or tea after 6 p.m.? Are you overstimulating your mind by watching too much television? Are you working late on a regular basis so that there is not enough time to switch off from work? Are you getting enough exercise to compensate for a sedentary occupation or working with video screens? It is worth your while looking into this area as closely as possible so that you can eliminate any noxious stimuli that might prevent you from sleeping properly. Once you have had a few nights' good quality sleep, you will see that the world begins to look a brighter place and fear levels come down.

Period

Ladies, please mark those days when you have your period with a 'P' in this section. This will help you establish whether there is a connection between your menstruation and the severity of your fear problem. In order to get a true picture you should keep your diary for at least three period cycles, preferably longer. As periods are influenced by your emotional responses to external events (be they good or bad), you will need several months to get reliable information.

For all the male readers and those women who are sure that their period has nothing to do with their fear, keep the diary for a minimum of one month, better still for two. If you find it hard to keep on jotting down notes, you can simplify it by looking at your day as a whole, rather than dividing it up into mornings, afternoons and evenings. It is better to simplify the diary in this way than not keep a diary at all.

Observing your own reactions is actually quite interesting; it is rather like doing a bit of detective work. You find out more about yourself and the way you think, and that is always an advantage when you are trying to solve a problem.

Let me give you a few examples that have been filled in by people with different fears and degrees of fears. In each case, I have picked out a typical week which illustrates the fear best. I will also give my comments at the end of each diary to help you interpret the notes.

Peter
26 years old, lives with his parents. Fear of social situations. See chart on pages 90 and 91.

Peter's notes show quite clearly how various incidents during the day affect his level of fear. It is interesting to see that a row with his mother ranks lower on his scale than less problematic situations with people at the office. He obviously feels better able to deal with a confrontation at home than with speaking to a colleague at work.

Even though there is no obvious reason to feel nervous on a Monday morning, Peter nevertheless rates his tension as 8 when he is only *thinking* about the day ahead.

Peter's sleep is not good as a result of being tense and worried, and as a consequence he doesn't feel refreshed when he wakes up the next morning. This leads to him feeling physically low and makes him more sensitive and therefore more vulnerable to stress.

Olivia
*70 years old, widowed, lives on her own. Agoraphobia –
can only leave house with her shopping trolley to hold on
to. See chart on pages 92 and 93.*

You can see that, in contrast to Peter's diary, Olivia's notes
show a much more random occurrence of high level fear. It is
often on a high figure in the mornings, even when there are no
particularly worrying events scheduled for the day. (However,
that does not mean that Olivia is not anticipating in her
thoughts that something worrying *might* happen during the
day!)

Equally, there does not seem any logical explanation for the
low level anxiety on Saturday. It is easy to see how this state of
affairs can be very disturbing. It almost appears as if the fear is a
thing in itself that strikes at random and stays away at random.

Olivia's sleep is generally bad, and even though she is
seventy years old, it is not enough to be only sleeping three to
four hours a night. When discussing this with her in detail, I
found that she always has the radio on when she goes to bed
and that she usually falls asleep with it still on. An hour or so
later, the sound wakes her up again. She decided to try out
keeping the radio switched off half an hour before she put the
lights out, and she found that her sleep improved and she could
eventually average five hours sleep per night.

CORRECT BREATHING AND
RELAXATION
Self-help
For all types of fear

Whenever you are afraid, your breathing gets shallower and
faster and your body tenses up. This mechanism happens without fail and quite automatically, and we are not even always
aware of this tension unless it is quite pronounced. We may be
worried about a situation at work, but it is only in the evening
that we realize that our neck hurts. However, when we feel
particularly anxious about a visit to the dentist, we are usually

Peter

Day	Fear level morn/aft/evg		Events	Physical symptoms	Mental/ emotional symptoms	Coping strategies	Sleep	Period
	morn	8	having to face people in the office for another week's work	'butterflies' in stomach; heartbeat faster	don't want to eat; problems concentrating at work	trying to distract my mind by thinking about next weekend	bad because worried	
MON	aft	7	need to ask colleague for help with my project					
	evg	2	back to safety at home!					
	morn	6	nervous about going to work	butterflies; tingling in palms of hands; sweating	problems speaking clearly; problems concentrating	trying to take deep breaths to calm down	not good	
TUE	aft	8	boss addresses mistake I made					
	evg	5	still thinking about mistake					
	morn	7	having to face boss again. Others are laughing – about me?	butterflies; generally tense	suspicious about others; feel like an outsider	–	can't go to sleep for a long time	
WED	aft	5	boss is not around; others leave me alone					
	evg	4	row at home with mother	evg: tense				

THU	morn	5	boss not in			—	sleeping, but waking up tired
	aft	4	all's calm at the office, nobody wants anything	morn and aft: not too bad, just slightly tense			
	evg	4	tense atmosphere at home. Should I move out?	evg: tense	annoyed that mother is so unreasonable		
FRI	morn	6	boss is back	very tense; sweating	very difficult to concentrate; tongue-tied		exhausted, sleeping like a log
	aft	8	new girl in office. Would love to speak to her but don't have the courage.			withdrawing	
	evg	2	things sorted out at home				
SAT	morn	3	weekend!	OK	relieved; relaxed	—	good
	aft	3	weekend!				
	evg	2	–				
SUN	morn	2	I'm bored but feel safe at home			—	not so good, worried about the next day
	aft	5	weekend nearly over	tension building up towards evg	starting to think about work again, about having to face the people in the office		
	evg	7	weekend is over				

Olivia

Day	Fear level morn/aft/evg		Events	Physical symptoms	Mental/ emotional symptoms	Coping strategies	Sleep	Period
MON	morn	8	nothing in particular	palpitations, feeling faint, trembling	anxious, confused, feeling out of control	–	restless, only four hours sleep	
	aft	8	nothing in particular why am I feeling like this?					
	evg	5	nothing in particular					
TUE	morn	7	nothing	palpitations in the morning, easing off when son rings	anxious in the morning, but very happy when family is there	–	not good	
	aft	6	son rang, will be coming over with family in the evening – have to go shopping					
	evg	3	visitors – pleasant!					
WED	morn	8	nothing	usual morning palpitations, faintness and trembling	feeling out of control and exasperated with it; depressed	distracting myself by getting jobs done in the garden. Works quite well.	good (very tired after garden work), only four hours sleep though.	
	aft	4	gardening: working three hours					
	evg	4	resting					
	morn	7	forcing myself to go to coffee morning; feel silly with shopping trolley	palpitations, faintness and trembling	fed up with my fear, decide to fight it. It's hard though!	making myself confront my fear. Didn't enjoy my outing, but at	restless; only three hours sleep	

THU	aft	6	housework				least it got me out of the house and I know I can still do it.
	evg	6	nothing in particular				
	morn	7	must go shopping today	palpitations get worse when going out, very tense, feeling exhausted by the time I get home	irritated, discontented, out of control, depressed	making myself confront my fear	OK. Slept five hours (!)
FRI	aft	8	going to supermarket				
	evg	5	glad to be back home!				
SAT	morn	6	nothing in particular	only light palpitations, feeling	confused. Why am I not afraid today?	—	restless; three hours
	aft	4	going for a walk, enjoying it! why aren't I nervous?	relatively calm when going for my walk	Enjoying it while it lasts.		
	evg	2	friend rings				
SUN	morn	8	nothing in particular	palpitations, trembling, feeling faint, tense	depressed	feeling lonely, so I make an effort to contact someone	restless; three hours
	aft	6	ringing a friend and having a chat				
	evg	6	nothing in particular				

aware of the physical tension straight away – the body seems 'locked', the heart is racing, the mouth is dry, the hands are sweaty and we have 'butterflies' in the stomach.

This knock-on effect between thoughts and physical reactions is also known as the body-mind link. Whatever goes on in the mind will be reflected in the body, and vice versa. If you witness an upsetting scene, for example two people having a violent row, your body will automatically tense up, even if you are merely watching this event on a cinema screen! The *degree* of tension is likely to differ depending on whether the row happens in reality or on a screen, but the fact remains that *your body will still react* as a consequence of what you perceive.

The same interdependence between body and mind becomes apparent should there be anything wrong with your body. If your kidneys are not functioning properly, you will feel more on edge and think more negatively. If you have an upset stomach you will find it harder to concentrate at work. This means, in other words, that the link can work both ways – the body can influence the mind, and the mind can influence the body.

When we transfer this knowledge onto a fear-related problem, we can see that this allows us two angles of attack. We can either work on getting rid of the fear and thereby ensure that the physical tension normalizes, or we turn the physical tension into relaxation and in this way reduce or even eliminate the fear. Ideally, one would tackle the fear problem from both angles, and in consequent chapters you will encounter examples for both mental and physical problem solving.

In this chapter, I am particularly concerned with the most fundamental of physical functions, namely our breathing. We breathe constantly, whether we are awake or asleep, whether we are aware of it or not. We don't need to know how we do it because our sympathetic nervous system is programmed to do it for us, and because it is all taken care of without any conscious efforts on our part, we are rarely aware of *how* we are breathing. Think about it for a moment. Do you really know exactly which parts of your body extend as you breathe in? Are you aware of how deep or shallow your breathing is and how it varies when you are sitting from when you are rushing around at work or when you are in the supermarket? Chances are that you are unable to answer any of these questions, and why should you?

If it is all working by itself, why waste time paying attention to your breathing?

Under normal circumstances, I could not agree with you more. It is only when you have a tension-related problem that it is necessary to pay some attention to your breathing.

Even though our breathing processes work on auto-pilot most of the time, we can certainly manipulate them. You may experience are such an occasion when you are about to dive under water in a pool and you hold your breath for a while, or you are going through an area out in the open where there is a bad smell in the air in which case you either hold your breath or breathe in a very shallow manner to avoid taking in too much of the offending smell. When, on the other hand, we want to take in the pleasant scent of flowers more intently, we lean over them and take a deep breath. So we are perfectly capable of manipulating our breathing, and we might as well harness this ability for our own purposes.

When you are relaxed and you are breathing calmly, you cannot at the same time be fearful. Fear can only exist in connection with a tightened body and quickened breathing. When you become very anxious, a natural physical reaction is to increase the rate and the depth of breathing. This phenomenon is also known as *hyperventilation*. When you 'over-breathe', you take in more oxygen, but at the same time you also expel more carbon dioxide, and the latter causes changes in blood chemistry which create a variety of symptoms such as lightheadedness, tingling and numbness in fingers and hands, muscle cramps and increased anxiety. If at this point you can manage to relax and normalize your breathing, the fear will abate.

There are various techniques for regulating your breathing and achieving a state of physical relaxation. These techniques are amazingly simple, but that does not mean that they are necessarily easy to carry out. Each and every one of the following methods needs to be practised on a regular basis and over a period of several weeks if you want to use them to combat fear successfully. Should your fear problem be particularly severe, practise your preferred method several times a day.

The rule of thumb is that the more pronounced your fear, the longer and more intensely you should do the breathing exercise. It is a bit like brainwashing your body into a different reaction to fear-inducing situations, so you will have to consistently disrupt the old tension pattern and replace it with the new relaxation pattern.

The principal muscle of respiration is the *diaphragm* which is a dome shaped membrane structure that separates the chest area from the abdomen. As the diaphragm contracts, the chest volume increases, thus lowering the internal pressure and causing the inspiration of air. As the diaphragm relaxes and expands, the air is expelled again from the lungs. The diaphragm is also involved in coughing, sneezing, crying or expelling urine and faeces.

In order to locate your diaphragm, put your hand on your stomach area, fingers slightly apart, with the little finger just above the navel. It is roughly where your thumb rests, near the breastbone, where the diaphragm has its highest point. From here, it continues down the lower ribs on both sides.

In order for the diaphragm to work properly, you need to give it room and elasticity to move freely. This means that tight clothing, in particular tight belts or waistbands, should be avoided. Another impediment to proper breathing is bad posture. If you slouch when you sit or stand, or if you are in the habit of letting your shoulders collapse forward, you physically limit the space available to your lungs to expand properly. Should you have problems with your posture, you might want to consult an Alexander Technique teacher who will help you correct the fault.

But back to your diaphragm. Leave your hand where you positioned it to find the diaphragm and we can go straight into the first breathing exercise.

Basic breathing exercise

1. With your hand on the area above your navel, tighten up your stomach and belly muscles so that they tuck in. Hold the tension for a moment.
2. Now let the muscles relax and feel the difference.
3. Repeat steps 1 and 2. You are now beginning to become aware of what the difference between tension and relaxation in that area feels like.

4. Now breathe in through the nose in such a way that your hand is being pushed up by the inflated stomach and belly region. Hold your breath for a moment.
5. Now breathe out through the mouth and notice how your stomach and belly deflate and how this makes your hand go down again.
6. Repeat steps 4 and 5 twenty times and notice how you become progressively calmer as you are doing this exercise.

I refer to this exercise as basic because it deals with one of the most common mistakes we make when breathing: we only use the top part of our lungs, the part that sits underneath the collar bones. At the same time, we keep the stomach and belly areas rigid and tight so that they won't expand, thereby preventing the lungs underneath from filling up with air.

By tensing and relaxing these neglected areas in steps 1 and 2, you become aware of what it feels like to let go of tension, and by letting your hand ride up and down with your breathing, you learn to harmonize your breathing and, as a consequence, induce greater calmness in your body.

If you find yourself getting nervous about something or you find a fear creeping up on you, put your hand on your stomach immediately and start breathing properly. That way you will be able to control the fear much better, and often you will find that you can make the fear disappear.

Counting breaths

This exercise is based on the previous one. It sounds deceptively simple, but it requires a lot of concentration to carry it out.

1. Close your eyes.
2. Breathe in so your stomach and belly areas rise up, then breathe out and, in your mind, count '1'. *Keep your attention on your breathing only, don't let other thoughts intrude.*
3. Continue breathing in and out, and each time you breathe out, count the next number in your mind. *Concentrate on your breathing only, don't let your mind wander off.*

What number did you get to before you found your mind wandering off? I don't mind telling you that initially I didn't get past number 2 before I drifted off into contemplations about the washing up, an unpaid bill or a problem at work . . .

Here are some tips that might make it easier to get into the higher figures.

a) When you say a number in your mind, *see* it at the same time, like the numbers of floors that illuminate on the panel of a lift. Hang on to that picture in your mind until you exhale the next time, then replace the number by the next one. That way you hold your attention on one particular thing which takes up space in your mind, thereby preventing other thoughts from taking over that space.

b) Another way of concentrating on what you are doing is to focus intently on the various sensations and movements that happen in the trunk of your body while you are breathing in and out. You will be surprised at all the details you can perceive and at how these details occur in a set pattern.

Counting breaths not only helps you regulate your breathing, it also has an effect on your mental state. As you concentrate on your breathing, you automatically clear your mind of other thoughts, in particular of unpleasant or fearful ones. This means that you can now begin to relax and unwind so that not just your body relaxes, but your mind also begins to feel restful. This in turn helps you go to sleep more easily when your mind is still buzzing with the day's events and problems. As you systematically work on achieving a physical and mental state which allows you to switch off, you create all the conditions you need to fall asleep.

Doing either of the breathing exercises will automatically result in the rest of the body beginning to relax, too. You are now ready to deepen the physical relaxation aspect even more by using one of the following exercises.

Fractional relaxation

'Fractional' in this context means that you are relaxing your body gradually and in individual steps.

1. Sit down or lie down. If you are sitting, make sure you can rest your head comfortably against the back of the chair, or put a cushion against the wall and lean against that. If you have no support and you have to hold your head in position, it will be difficult to relax the neck muscles, and they are one of the most common stress areas.
2. Close your eyes so you can concentrate better on what you are doing.
3. Start off by slowly tensing the muscles in your feet until you have a clear feeling of tension in them. Hold the tension for a moment so that you can be fully aware of it. Now let the tension go very slowly. If you are lying down, let your feet flop loosely outwards when you relax them.
4. Now concentrate on your calf muscles. Tense them up slowly and while you do so, try to disturb other muscles as little as possible. Hold the tension for a moment. Now release the muscles again slowly until they are as relaxed as they can be.
5. Continue in the same manner in the following order: thighs, belly area, chest area, hands, arms, shoulders and neck together, face (frown and clench your teeth).
6. Rest a little while after you have completed the exercise so that you can enjoy the full benefit of relaxation.

The skill in this exercise is in doing it very deliberately, paying a great deal of attention to what the various parts of the body feel like when they are tensing up, while they are suspended in tension for a moment, while they are in the process of relaxing and when they are finally completely relaxed.

When you have finished the entire exercise, be aware of the sense of physical relaxation, and also notice what your individual relaxation signs are. Some people experience a sense of heaviness in the limbs or in the entire body, other people feel quite light, as if they were floating. Notice how your breathing has become quieter and more regular; notice how the thoughts in your mind have slowed down. Other signs of relaxation are little muscle jerks (just like the ones you might sometimes get when you are about to fall asleep) and little gurgling sounds in your stomach.

Visualization

Another, more indirect way to relax the body is via a mental image. This image has to be tailor-made to your needs, so in order to find your ideal image, sit down for a moment and quietly think to yourself the sentence 'A serene and quiet and safe place where I can be calm and relaxed'. Wait a moment, then repeat the thought again and see which image presents itself to you. You might have a spontaneous idea, or you might have to let your mind drift over a variety of possibilities and select the one that you find yourself most drawn to. Here are a few ideas for places indoors or outdoors that you might want to consider:

- a little room overlooking beautiful countryside
- a penthouse flat with a room that is high above the hustle and bustle of everyday life
- a cave in a beautiful mountainside, filled with rugs and cushions so you can be comfortable
- a tropical beach with fine golden sand
- a romantic garden filled with flowers and beautiful trees, the fragrance of the flowers drifting through the air
- a green hillside with views in all directions
- a seat underneath an old willow tree by a lovely lake

The possibilities are endless! It doesn't have to be a place that actually exists; the nice thing about this image is that you can make it up as you go along.

Once you have settled for one image, proceed as follows.

1. Sit or lie down comfortably and close your eyes.
2. Bring up the image of your place and pretend you are in this place.
3. Begin to explore this place visually. What can you see? Take in as much detail as you can. If, for example, you have chosen a beach, look at the palm trees and the pattern their fronds make against the sky; look at the sand, the sea; look at the pattern that the waves create in the sand as they roll onto the beach; watch how the sea water oozes away into the sand; look at the little crests of white on top of the waves; be aware of the colour of the sky and the sea.
4. Also immerse yourself in the sounds of your environment,

like the sounds as the waves rolling in; the slight hissing sounds as the waves recede; birds in the trees; the sound of the palm tree fronds in the breeze.

5. Also imagine any tactile sensations, like the feel of the fine sand under your feet; the feel as you take a handful of sand and let it run through your fingers; walking on wet sand by the water edge; feeling little waves roll over your feet.

6. Hold that image and all the sensations that go with it as long as possible in your mind. Imagine you are on holiday here for months on end and there is absolutely nothing you need to do here. Nobody wants anything and nobody expects anything, so you can *really* relax.

7. Check for relaxation signs once you open your eyes again (heaviness, more comfortable beathing and so on).

It is a good idea to combine at least two of the exercises. You could do the fractional relaxation first and then go into your image, or you can do one of the breathing exercises and couple that with the fractional or the visualization exercise.

All the exercises have a cumulative effect. The more you practise, the easier they become and the more quickly you will achieve relaxation.

PHYSICAL EXERCISE
Self-help
For all types of fear, but for panic attacks please read special note on page 106

You may be surprised to find a section on exercising in a book about fear. Many people think of anxiety as being a purely mental or emotional process that has a detrimental effect on your psychological well-being. However, the fact is that any fear problem has also a direct negative effect on your body. As there is a direct link between mind and body, any experience of fear will automatically involve the body and cause a multitude of reactions as we have seen in earlier chapters – you tense up, you sweat, your pulse rate goes up, your heart races, you have butterflies in your stomach, you clench your jaw muscles and your hands get tingly, to name just a few. When you experience fear on a regular basis, you get into a state of continual emotional upheaval, and that leads to an inability to relax physically. But the higher your physical tension level, the more likely it is that you will experience another bout of fear; in other words, the physical symptoms which are created by your fear help perpetuate that very fear. It is a vicious circle that makes it difficult for you to get away from your fear.

Physical exercise is therefore a very important step in resolving your fear. You will still need to use mental techniques to complement your fitness programme, but you will find it a great deal easier, for example, to mentally relax if your body is thoroughly relaxed first. *Mens sana in corpore sano*, as the ancient Romans knew – a healthy mind in a healthy body.

I am aware that you may now begin to have nightmarish visions of yourself with all your excess pounds squeezed into an ungainly leotard, looking red in the face as you jump up and down amongst a class of super-lithe nymphettes ... Or you may be concerned that you will do damage to yourself or head for a heart attack if you start exercising now, when the most strenuous sporting activity you have done in the last few years has been to watch Wimbledon or the FA Cup finals on television ... Please don't worry; there are gentle ways of launching yourself into a fitness programme that suits your needs.

If you have not exercised in a long time, especially if you are over forty, I would recommend you speak to your GP first. You will need to make sure that your heart is OK and that you don't suffer from diabetes or conditions like arthritis that may be aggravated by exercise. Are your knees and ankles ever a problem? Is your spine OK or do you have problems with discs sometimes? Do you suffer from high blood pressure? Do you have chest problems like asthma or bronchitis? Are you pregnant? All these conditions will make it necessary for you to ask for medical advice; they don't, however, mean that you cannot set up an exercise routine for yourself. You will just have to choose more carefully what sort of exercises you can do and you may have to restrict yourself to certain sports and follow some special guidelines. Nowadays, many modern fitness centres offer an initial consultation where they check your fitness level and double check with you on any health problems you might have, so that could be a good starting point.

One simple way of checking your level of fitness is to check your *resting pulse*. When you feel reasonably relaxed, place your fingers (not your thumb!) on the inside of your wrist and press very gently until you can feel the pulse. With the help of a watch which shows the seconds, count the pulse beats you have within one minute. Very roughly, if you count 80 pulse beats or more in one minute, your state of fitness definitely requires improvement; if it is between 70 and 80, you may need more exercise; if it is below 70, you are probably in quite good shape. These ratings are obviously all relative, and there will be individual deviations. One person's ideal resting rate may be 65, whereas the next person may only get down to 75 on exactly the same training programme.

Before looking into various exercises in more detail, let me explain more about what the physical benefits are. Provided you exercise regularly, you will positively affect your body and thereby create a feeling of well-being. Your muscles relax after the exercises (even though they might ache initially); adrenalin is used up which brings down your emotional tension level; the production of endorphines, the body's 'feel-good' substances, is increased; your circulation and metabolism improve; your energy levels increase (even though you may feel tired during and for a short while after exercising); your cholesterol levels and blood pressure come down and your blood sugar levels become better balanced. As a consequence, you feel on a more even keel, you sleep better and you feel more in control – and therefore less anxious.

There are a great number of exercise ideas to choose from. Here is a selection of options:

brisk walking, jogging, running, running on the spot, skipping rope, trampolining, weight training, aerobics, swimming, horse riding, rowing, cycling, ice skating, roller skating, skiing, tennis, football, squash, basketball, volleyball

What you choose depends on whether you prefer to work out in the privacy of your own home or whether you would rather join a class. Some people find they cannot be bothered to set out again once they have come home from work in the evenings, so they buy a video and follow a programme at home. On the other hand, you may find that you need the motivation of a group to get going, or you may enjoy the social aspects of exercising, so you would go for a sport that involves other people.

Once you have chosen one or possibly two different options (you can combine different sports for your training pro-gramme), and if you are reasonably fit, do a trial session to assess where your fitness boundary lies. Say, for example, you have chosen swimming. How many lengths can you do before you are out of breath? If you have chosen aerobics, how long can you keep up with the rest of the class (or the video) until you have to stop? Your body will give you clear indications of when it has had enough. Listen to it! – You now have a lowest mark which you can work on improving from now on.

Should you be totally unfit, that is if you are puffing and panting if you have to walk up a flight of stairs, you may need to start at an easier level. Brisk walking can help you build up cardiovascular conditioning. Again, start off by checking how many minutes you can walk energetically before you are out of breath. In order to derive a beneficial effect from your walking you will have to increase it to at least 30 minutes. Once you have reached this minimum level and maintained it for at least five days in a row, you should be able to go on to a different sort of exercise category, maybe slow jogging or running on the spot, or any other sport that appeals to you.

Here are some tips that will make it easier for you to embark on your exercise programme.

1. *Always make sure you wear the right footwear* when you engage in a sport that involves your feet. Get advice if necessary. Your feet should be well cushioned and the ankles and heels firmly supported when you do any form of running or jumping.
2. *Start slowly.* Do a trial session and establish your present limit. Increase your limit gradually. Be patient. Don't expect to jog around the block today and run a marathon tomor-row.
3. *Exercise at least four times a week.* Get into a routine, make exercise part of your daily timetable if you can. You won't reap any benefits, certainly not with regard to reducing fear, if you exercise only once a week.
4. *Persist.* When you start off, the benefits may well be over-

shadowed by aching muscles and tiredness, but as you progress, those initial negative side-effects will begin to disappear and give way to higher energy levels and greater well-being.

5. *Reward yourself initially to keep yourself going.* In the beginning, coax yourself into keeping up the routine by allowing yourself little treats after you have done the exercise. Later, you will find that you are actually looking forward to exercising, so the exercise itself becomes the reward.

6. *Start now.* Start organizing yourself. Find out about classes or buy a video, get the right clothes out or buy them and get going as soon as possible. Believe me – there is no such thing as the 'right time'; don't wait for it, it may never come, and meanwhile you are stuck with your fear. Do you really want to hang on to it longer than necessary?

7. *Make a contract with yourself.* As it will take about four weeks of exercising at least four times a week before you get tangible results concerning your fear problem, you will have to commit yourself to doing the exercises properly, regularly and persistently. So here is your contract!

CONTRACT

I, ... , confirm that I am a person with a will and a mind of my own and that I am fed up with my fear. I have therefore decided to do something constructive about it.

I promise to carry out my fitness programme at least four times a week for a minimum of four weeks.

Week 1 ☐ ☐ ☐ ☐ ☐ ☐ ☐

Week 2 ☐ ☐ ☐ ☐ ☐ ☐ ☐

Week 3 ☐ ☐ ☐ ☐ ☐ ☐ ☐

Week 4 ☐ ☐ ☐ ☐ ☐ ☐ ☐

. . . .
Date   Signature

---

8. *Warm up*. Never launch into *any* exercise without having spent a few minutes shaking out your limbs, stretching arms and legs and generally loosening up. Your muscles need a bit of time to get into gear; this way you get them ready so that they can function to their fullest extent.

9. *Don't exercise when you are ill*. When you are not feeling well, your body needs all its strength to combat the illness, so if you use up your strength by exercising during that time it will take you longer to get over the illness, or in some cases, can even aggravate it.

10. *Stop exercising if you feel a sudden or sharp pain anywhere*. If the pain persists, get it checked out.

11. *Increase your upper limit*. In order to get really fit you need to progress past your initial limit. Do that at your own pace, but do it. You want to build up stamina because that will help you build confidence and reduce fear. Check your resting pulse rate weekly (see p. 103); until it comes down to an acceptable level, you still need to increase your upper exercise limit.

Believe me, it's all worth it! Trust my experience – this is an ex-couch-potato speaking . . .

Special note for panic attack sufferers

Be particularly gentle in building up your training programme. Some physical effects you get from exercising may remind you of physical effects that occur with panic attacks, and this might initially confuse you. Be aware that your breathing rate naturally increases as you exercise your body, so there is no need to worry about it.

DESENSITIZATION THROUGH VISUALIZATION
Self-help and therapy
For simple phobias, social phobias and fear of performance

In order to use this method successfully, you will have to have practised relaxation and correct breathing first; so if you have come straight to this section, please go back to those earlier sections and work through them or you will lack the necessary basic skills for visualization.

Desensitization means a gradual approaching of a situation or object that has induced fear in the past. If you use desensitization in connection with visualization, it means that you take a step-by-step approach towards your aim by using the powers of your imagination. You do this by visualizing in your mind how you perform the various steps before trying them out in reality.

The advantage of desensitization through visualization is that you can experiment from the safety of your armchair until you feel physically calm whilst performing a certain step, and only then do you attempt to carry out that step in reality.

In order to visualize well, you need to relax first of all. Use any of the methods you practised in the section about correct breathing and relaxation.

Visualization is the language of the subconscious mind, and it is a very powerful language indeed. Whatever you spend a lot of time visualizing will eventually come true, and that goes for positive and for negative images!

To visualize means to see something in your mind's eye. We do this quite naturally every day without realizing that we are doing so. Try it out on someone else. Ask them what *their* living room looks like while they are sitting in yours. Observe them closely. You will see how they first look away from you and stare into space, or they may look at you but somehow *through* you as they are describing their room. They may also move their head in various directions or point with their hands as they are outlining where things are in their living room. What they are doing at that moment is to *look at their own living room in their mind* – hence the far away look in their eyes.

Ask them what colour their sofa is and watch how they stare at a spot in your room as they mentally look at their sofa, possibly narrowing their eyes to concentrate better and 'see' it more clearly and then give you an answer. In other words, they are looking at something that isn't there in reality but only exists as a picture in their mind.

We all have mental images in our mind of all the things we know, and we can look at these mental pictures to access the information we need, even if the actual items are not there in reality. This is what we call visualization.

Seeing with your mind's eye can be different from 'normal' seeing. Whereas, in everyday life, we can see things very distinctly and with a clearly defined shape and with distinguishable colours, we may only see things vaguely and blurred in our own mind's eye. Visualization can sometimes feel like having an *idea* in your mind rather than an actual picture.

Should you find that your visualization skills leave something to be desired, don't worry — you can train your imagining faculties quite easily.

Think about a building you know well, perhaps your house or your office. Close your eyes, relax and then go on a mental journey. Look at the entrance in your mind, walk inside, go through the various rooms, look at the furniture and the furnishings, go to your room, notice how you open the door (is it a door handle or a door knob? *Look* at it!) and sit down in the most comfortable seat in your room. Look at the seat, feel the material of the seat, look out of the window and notice what you see. If you want to, you can speak out loud and describe what you see in your mind if that helps convince you that you *do* see something in your mind.

There are not many people who can get a life-like, sharply focused image in their mind, so don't expect to experience something like a cinema film. *This is not necessary anyway*. As long as you can describe to someone else what you have just imagined, your visualization is good enough to be used for desensitization.

Should you have any problems with this exercise, spend some time *in reality* looking at your house from the outside. Start paying attention to detail. What colour is the front door? Which side is the lock on and what does it feel like when you insert the key in the lock? If there are several locks, notice which one you open first. As you go through the front door, notice what it is you see first as you step through the doorway. Once inside your house, sit down, close your eyes and re-run all these details in your mind.

If you find this exercise still too complex, simplify it even further. Look at everyday objects, such as your watch, your telephone, a framed picture or a particular chair in your room and take your time to really concentrate on it for a few minutes. Then close your eyes and try to recall the details. When you have 'seen' all the details that you can remember, open your eyes and check whether your mental image was correct or whether you missed out on something. You will be surprised at how little you know about objects that you look at every day. For example, could you say whether your watch has dots or strokes or figures for the hours? ... (No cheating, don't look straight away, really try to remember.) ... An amazing number of people are unable to give you that information about their own watch. Try it out on others!

Once you have practised your visualization for a while and you are satisfied with your mental imagery, you need to break down your goal into smaller steps. I call this the *achievement ladder*.

Let us assume that you would like to overcome a social phobia, for example attending parties. On the scale from one to ten, your aim could be to be relaxed and confident at parties or even to be able to organize a party yourself.

Your complete achievement ladder could look as follows:

Fear of attending social events

0. Cannot go to parties at all.
1. Able to think about parties without getting nervous.
2. Attending a party for a short while, speaking to one or two people you know.
3. Attending a party for a short while, staying relaxed while speaking to one or two people you know.
4. Attending a party, staying relaxed while speaking to people you know and listening to people you don't know.
5. Relaxed with people you know, relaxed listening to people you don't know.
6. Able to answer adequately when approached by a person you don't know.
7. Able to approach one person you don't know and start a very short conversation with them.
8. Able to approach several people you don't know and start a conversation with them.

9. Relaxed and confident at parties.
10. Organizing a party yourself and enjoying it.

As you can see, the individual steps are quite close together. The only difference between steps 2 and 3 is that in step 2 you do something whereas in step 3 you are relaxed doing it. This sort of grading gives you a chance to be *not perfect*, and that is very important. Many people give up too easily because they may be at step 4 and want to be at 10. Naturally, that is far too large a gap to bridge quickly. If, however, you divide up the remaining distance to your aim into smaller, more manageable steps of improvement, the successful achievement of your goal becomes more easily attainable.

Here is another example of an achievement ladder.

Fear of leaving the house

0. Refusing to go out, avoiding talking or thinking about it.
1. Remaining calm while thinking about opening the front door and looking outside.
2. Remaining calm while taking a couple of steps away from the front door.
3. Being calm and relaxed while remaining a couple of steps away from the front door and staying there for three minutes.
4. Walking down to the next street corner and back.
5. Remaining calm while walking to the next street corner and back.
6. Going to nearby little shop (*not* supermarket) and buying one item and immediately returning home.
7. Going to nearby little shop, buying something and dawdling on the way back home, looking at gardens or shop windows.
8. Going a longer distance away to buy something in a larger shop (supermarket or department store).
9. Going a longer distance away to buy something, going to two shops and dawdling on the way back home.
10. Leaving the house without thinking about it being a problem.

You may well find that you do not have to start from step 1 if you have already progressed to a later step on the achievement ladder by using your own strategies. You also don't have to section your achievement ladder into ten steps — it may make more sense in your case to only break it down into six or eight steps. What matters is that the steps are small enough to be achieveable.

Now you have your two main ingredients for desensitization ready: visualization and the achievement ladder. Start with the step that presents the lowest degree of difficulty for you. In the party example, let us assume you have avoided parties for quite a while, so you now have to start from the bottom rung with step 1.

However, before you start visualizing, ALWAYS ALWAYS ALWAYS do a relaxation exercise first. The visualization will only be effective if you do it while in a relaxed state.

To give you an example, I will now take you step by step through the visualizations for our first example on page 109.

Visualization for step 1

After having relaxed, let a picture come to your mind of a party. Make sure you are not in the picture but just watching it from the outside, as if the picture was on a screen. Watch people milling about, talking, laughing, drinking, some people noisier than others, some people listening more than talking.

Visualization for step 2

Create in your mind a similar picture to the above. This time, imagine yourself joining the party on the periphery, just for a short time, speaking a little to a couple of people you know, maybe waving briefly to someone else you know and then leaving again. It is OK if this visualization is coupled with a feeling of being somewhat rushed or not very interested.

Initially, be outside the image and watch it on a screen. When you can do this, go into the screen and try out what it feels like being *in* the picture.

Visualization for step 3

Same as step 2, but change the feeling to one of being happy to see these people. Also make sure to see that *they* are pleased to see you, asking you questions that you can answer easily, and you asking them questions with genuine interest. Feel inside that animated feeling of actually enjoying this communication, even though you have only popped in for a short while.

Do this first from outside the screen, then go inside.

Visualization for step 4

Same as step 3, but add another little scenario to your image. Find yourself listening quietly, without any comments, to what another group of people are discussing. If necessary, do this first from outside the screen and then go inside. If, however, you have now gathered enough confidence, go straight into the screen.

Visualization for step 5

Same as step 4, but add the element of relaxation to it. Introduce a relaxed posture into your image; see yourself sinking back comfortably into a chair and taking up space with your body. If you imagine yourself standing up, lean against a mantlepiece or a doorframe, maybe with a drink in your hand.

Be outside the screen or go immediately inside it, depending on how confident you feel.

Visualization for step 6

Same as step 5 but add an extra scenario of someone whom you don't know approaching you. Imagine that they start up a conversation with you and picture the two of you having a little chat. Make this scene fairly short (imagine the unknown person soon getting sidetracked by an old friend in the crowd).

Visualization for step 7

Now reverse step 6. Imagine that it is you who is approaching someone you don't know. You may have heard from a friend that you have a hobby in common with the unknown person. This makes it easy to speak to them because you can be sure that you will get the conversation going in a relaxed manner. Go through all the motions in detail in your mind, addressing the other person, asking questions, answering questions and concluding the conversation.

Visualization for step 8

Same as step 7, but make it a little group of unknown people.

Visualization for step 9

Make this step a summary of all the previous steps and make sure you get a very positive, relaxed feeling as you experience the image, feeling comfortable with every aspect of the party. Talk, dance, laugh, and have a good time.

Visualization for step 10

Imagine that you enjoy parties so much that you have decided to organize one yourself. Go through all the details in your mind, inviting the guests, organizing food and drink, greeting people at the door, making introductions, having a good time yourself.

In the party achievement ladder, I have given you a very wide range between step 1 and step 10. When you set up your personal achievement ladder, you will not necessarily go to these extremes. You may not be a party person at all but have to attend some of them, so really all you want to do is be able to go to these social occasions and feel in control. In this case you would not need to take your ladder beyond step 6 or 7.

Any visualization needs to be tested against reality, otherwise you won't know how far you have come in the desensitization process. This does not mean that you have to go to a party for every visualization step you take. However, it would be useful, once you have arrived at step 4 for example, to go out and test it, and then test again when you feel comfortable with step 6.

With our other example of an achievement ladder on p. 110 (fear of leaving the house), testing should occur with every single step. When you have successfully tested a particular step, make sure you repeatedly perform this step in reality while you practise visualizing the next step. For example, if you have managed to go to the corner of your street and back again (step 5), you can go on to visualize going into a shop, but while you are working on step 6, keep making your little journeys down to the corner of your street. *Any successful first test has to be followed by several more practise runs to reinforce the new found skills.* You need to become used to your extended boundaries, and this means that you have to 'patrol' this new territory regularly to make it yours. Only when you have expanded your comfortable space and feel reasonably at home in it should you extend your space further.

Test your visualizations in your own time. Be thorough. Make sure you can cope with one step before you go on to the next, then practise the new step to build confidence, and only then proceed. Always remember that it doesn't matter how long it takes to get to your goal, as long as you get there.

NEURO-LINGUISTIC PROGRAMMING (NLP)
Self-help and therapy
For worrying, simple phobias, social phobias and fear of performance

NLP was started in the early seventies at the University of California by John Grinder and Richard Bandler who studied the work of Fritz Perls, the originator of Gestalt therapy, Virginia Satir, a family therapist, and Milton Erickson, a psychiatrist who used hypnosis in his work.

Bandler and Grinder set out to identify the underlying patterns that made these three therapists so unusually successful, and then went on to create from these patterns models which could be taught and used both by individuals who wanted to improve certain areas of their life as well as by therapists who wanted an efficient tool to help their clients overcome problems.

NLP deals with the way we structure our subjective experiences in our mind, how we organize what we see, hear and feel and how we describe our experiences in language and how we act, consciously and unconsciously, to attain certain results.

Very much like positive thinking, NLP does not deal with the concept of failure – there is no such thing as failure, only results. If we find that we do not like the results we are getting, we need to find out how we can change our thinking or our beliefs or our concept of the world in order to obtain the results we want. The findings of NLP can give us many useful techniques which we are encouraged to tailormake to our own subjective needs, using our own subjective resources.

NLP has made a great number of valuable contributions to the resolution of fears and phobias, and it is these particular techniques that I would like to concentrate on now, even though NLP can help with a much wider field of symptoms.

One of my clients used to be very worried every time he had to give a talk or lecture. This would happen every two or three months so that he could never really get into a routine and lose his anticipatory fear through frequently experiencing a successful outcome. Even though he was always well prepared and his lectures had been well received in the past, he spent an agonizing week before every event, struggling with sleepless nights and self-doubts. On a conscious level, he knew that his worrying was superfluous, but on a subconscious level, he still experienced doubts, and as soon as his subconscious mind got the upper hand (which was usually when he lay in bed and was about to go to sleep), fearful thoughts and pictures would appear in his mind and disturb him.

After two years he became so fed up with this pattern that he decided to take action. Having come across NLP by then he did the following.

Initially, he sat down and, with closed eyes, imagined the

forthcoming seminar as a picture in his mind. This picture was like a photograph, and it showed an auditorium full of people with himself standing at the front, speaking. As he was looking at the photograph, he could already feel his heart beating faster and his stomach getting tied up in knots.

Now he began to manipulate that photograph in order to change the feeling of fear to a neutral feeling. In order to achieve this, he experimented with the seminar-image in his mind, at the same time closely observing his physical reactions. He began by making the image dimmer, fading and blurring the outlines; then he tried making the image smaller, moving it away into the distance. He also changed the image from colour to black and white, all the while monitoring any physical changes occurring in his body as he was watching the image in his mind.

After trying out these various approaches he found that when he turned the picture black and white and made it so small that it was only a black dot, he could change his feelings from anxious to neutral.

Once he had established what he needed to do, he used this technique continuously for several days. Whenever he caught himself thinking about the seminar and getting anxious, he interrupted his thoughts by closing his eyes, putting the black and white image in his mind and reducing it to a black dot, thus neutralizing the fear. As he kept doing this persistently, he noticed that he was sleeping better and generally thinking and worrying less about the seminar even though it was drawing nearer. As he realized that he could actually make his worries go away at will, his confidence increased and he observed how he was able to improve his performance even further, simply because he felt calmer and more relaxed.

Let us go through this process again step by step so you can reproduce it for yourself.

1. Sit or lie down and close your eyes.
2. Think about the situation that you are afraid of. Notice what image comes into your mind as you think about this situation.
3. Watch the image carefully. Notice how big it is, whether it is black and white or colour, notice some of the details in the

image, and above all, notice your feelings as you are looking at the image.

4. Now start manipulating the image. There are various things you can change about it:

    size – make it smaller or bigger

    brightness – make it dimmer or brighter

    distance – push it further away or bring it closer

    clarity – make it more blurred or more sharply focused

    location – push the image to the side or put it behind your head

    This list is not comprehensive. You may think of other ways to change the image visually.

5. If you associate certain sounds with your image, for example if you are afraid of dogs and associate the image of a dog with the sound of barking, you can change the sound in the following ways:

    volume – turn it down

    tone – make it softer

    clarity – make it more muffled

    speed – turn down the sound to 'slow motion'

    distance – make it be further away from you

Again, this list is not comprehensive but is just meant to give you the most common features. Feel free to try out new ideas; it if works for you, that is all that matters.

6. While you are experimenting with steps 4 and 5, observe closely which changes neutralize your physical feelings of fear best.

7. Establish which change or combination of changes result in the neutralizing of your fear. Now run through the procedure several times quite quickly – for example, whizz your image from its original size to a black dot over on your left hand side, or quickly dim your image down until it dissolves while at the same time turning down the volume all the way. Repeat the procedure five times, taking only one second for each repeat.

8. Now look at your original size picture again and check how you feel. You should now feel less anxious than before or, ideally, not anxious at all.

9. If there is still some anxiety, repeat step 7 until you can look at the original picture and feel neutral.

Our mind has a tendency to think and feel in certain patterns. We can learn to be afraid of a certain situation within a split second, and in that short moment, a pattern is established that is so profound and longlasting that it is triggered off for years after the original event. With NLP, we make use of our mind's ability to learn rapidly by redesigning that pattern at will and thereby restructuring the way we react and feel.

Another way of tackling fear with NLP is to change the image to something humorous.

Susan was afraid every time she had to go and visit an old aunt. This aunt had brought Susan up and had always been very strict. And even though all this was thirty years ago, my client felt herself retreating into child-mode every time she went back to see that aunt. When I asked Susan to think about her aunt, the image that came to her mind was that of approaching the aunt's glass maisonette door and seeing her aunt approaching the door from the inside. On closer inspection, it turned out that the aunt's image was that of a little old lady dressed in black. Just looking at that image in her mind, Susan said, made her feel extremely uncomfortable.

I asked her to bear with that feeling a little bit longer, to keep looking at the image and to do something with the image that resulted in her finding it amusing or funny. Susan spent a little while experimenting silently with her picture, and finally burst out laughing. It turned out that she had changed her aunt's clothing, put a checked shirt on her, dressed her in an orange mini-skirt and put green high-heeled lace-up boots on her spindly legs. The bigger she made that picture in her mind, the stronger her urge to laugh became. The ban was broken, and she told me later that whenever she went to see her aunt from then on, she really had to pull herself together not to burst out laughing . . .

In NLP, you can also work with mental films, rather than just still pictures. This can be very helpful when you deal with present phobias or past memories that make you feel uncomfortable. Let me give you an example. Let us assume you have a phobia of going in a lift.

1. Make yourself comfortable and close your eyes.

2. Imagine that you are sitting in a cinema and you are looking at the blank screen.

3. Now put a still, black and white picture onto the screen which shows the moment just before you enter a lift. While you keep the picture there, imagine yourself floating out of your body and floating up into the projection room of the cinema, so that you are now looking down at yourself, seeing yourself down there in your seat, watching yourself on the screen.

4. From the projection room, make the black and white picture on the screen into a film and watch the whole sequence of you getting into the lift, trembling and nervous. Watch yourself in the lift, sweating, looking awful, paralysed with fear, incapable of controlling yourself, until the lift comes to a halt and you can see yourself getting out. Hold the last picture there.

5. Now jump from the projection room into the screen and run the whole film backwards, as if you were rewinding it, with yourself in it. Make the film colour now, let everything go backwards, gestures, sounds and direction of movement. Do this *very quickly*, within one second.

6. Repeat the rewinding with yourself in the film another four times, very quickly each time.

7. Now wipe the screen blank and put the original black and white picture back on the screen and look at it from your seat in the cinema. Check how you feel as you are looking at the screen.

This process is known as the *Three Minute Phobia Cure* in NLP, and it appears to work by destroying the habitual fear pattern in the mind. By running the film backwards and by doing this very quickly, the trigger function of the initial image is confused and ultimately deleted.

This technique can also be used when a past event keeps bothering you or interferes with your life to an extent where it becomes disruptive. This can happen when something has gone wrong, where something embarrassing happened or where an uncomfortable situation occurred which you want to stop thinking about.

As an example, let us assume that you keep remembering

how you failed an important exam in the past. As a consequence you now feel anxious because you have lost confidence. If you are trying to build up new confidence, it can be very disruptive if the old failure memory crops up in your mind repeatedly.

In order to reprogramme your mind to wipe out the unpleasant feelings that go with this past event, follow the same steps as those for the Three Minute Phobia Cure. As you are putting the initial black and white picture on the screen, choose maybe the moment before you enter the exam room. From the projection room, watch the drama unfold as you are getting flustered in the film, not performing well because of your nerves, all the way through until you get your exam results and find that you have failed. Now jump into the film and run it backwards in colour; do this rapidly five times. Now check how you feel when you look at the original black and white picture and repeat the procedure until your feelings are in neutral.

With the Three Minute Phobia Cure, you may find that initially the neutralizing effect wears off to a certain extent. In that case, the only thing you need to do is to repeat the phobia cure procedure again, preferably immediately on realizing that an anxious feeling begins to recur. You will notice that the intensity and the frequency of the anxious feelings begin to wane quite rapidly as you keep bombarding your mind with confusing signals, so that finally the original trigger link between memory of the original event and the fear reaction has been obliterated.

One last NLP technique I would like to discuss here is the so-called *Swish*. This is another effective tool to combat fear, especially if you are clear about the feeling you would like to replace the fear with. When you work with the Swish, you use a positive feeling to blot out the negative feeling of fear.

One of my clients, Elizabeth, was due to get married for the second time. Her first marriage had been very unhappy and had ended acrimoniously, and even though her fiancé was an entirely different type of man from her first husband, she started having panic attacks at night, fearing that everything would go wrong again. On a rational level, she knew that the two of them could and would make things work, but her subconscious mind sent her very different messages at night!

I asked Elizabeth to give me a mental picture which was symbolic for her fear. She remembered sitting in a restaurant with her husband-to-be and some very good friends and feeling tongue-tied and anxious because of her doubts. I then asked her to put this picture onto a screen in her mind and feel all the feelings that went with looking at that picture.

Then I asked her to wipe the screen blank and put another picture of one time when she remembered feeling very sure about the forthcoming marriage. She remembered being in a little country church with her fiancé, looking out of the door onto a beautiful landscape outside and knowing deep in her heart that they could make the marriage work. I asked Elizabeth to put an image of that moment onto the screen and feel all the feelings that went with the event at the time. Once she had accessed these feelings of elation and confidence, I asked her to wipe the screen blank again.

Now she was asked to put the 'negative' picture of herself in the restaurant on the screen in black and white so that it filled the entire screen. Then she was to put the 'positive' picture of herself in the church in the top right hand corner of the screen, in colour, but very small. Now I asked her to swish the colour picture over the entire screen so that it blotted out the black and white picture underneath. She was to do this very quickly and tell me once she had done this.

Now she had to wipe the screen blank again and put the negative black and white image back, but this time making it smaller so that it would not fill the entire frame anymore. The positive colour picture was to go into the top right hand corner again. Now I asked Elizabeth to quickly swish the colour picture over the entire screen again and then make the colour picture really bright and give the colour brilliance.

We repeated this process several times, progressively making the negative picture smaller and the positive picture more vibrant and colourful. In the last sequence the negative picture was a mere spot on the screen.

Now I asked Elizabeth to imagine that she had a remote control with a test button, and that on pressing the test button, one of the two pictures would appear on the screen. She pressed the test button in her mind and immediately saw the positive colour picture on the screen. I then asked her to go into the screen and really feel what it was like to be sure and to be confident, then to come out of the screen and open her eyes again.

I told Elizabeth to remember the screen, and whenever she began to worry, to close her eyes and watch the last sequence of the little black spot in the middle of the screen which got washed away by the beautiful brilliant colour picture. Her panic attacks did not recur.

In this section, I have given you three different NLP techniques that are all very effective when applied properly. You will find that many different sorts of fears respond very positively to these methods.

Let yourself be guided by your own preference and use your imagination when you are working with your pictures.

Should you experience any problems carrying out NLP exercises, refer to the list at the end of this book for contact addresses to find an NLP therapist near you.

POSITIVE THINKING
Self-help and therapy
For worrying, simple phobias, social phobias, agoraphobia and fear of performance

Legend has it that many years ago there was a golden temple in India, right in the middle of a dense jungle. The temple was beautiful to behold, with its golden walls glittering in the sunshine. Inside, the temple was decorated with thousands of crystal mirrors.

One day a dog lost his way in the jungle and came across the temple. He admired the magnificent edifice and immediately considered himself the owner. When he entered the great hall with its thousands of mirrors, he suddenly saw himself faced with thousands of dogs who looked as fiercely at him as he was looking at them. As he was afraid that these dogs might steal away the temple's gold from him, he bared his teeth and started barking angrily. All the other dogs barked back at him, just as ferociously and angrily. This made the dog so furious that he ran up to attack one of the thousand dogs, crashed into the crystal mirrors and broke his neck.

Many years later, another dog lost his way in the jungle and came to the temple. When he entered the hall with the mirrors, he also found himself facing thousands of dogs. He was over-joyed to find so many of his kind in such a forlorn place and started happily wagging his tail, and all the other dogs wagged their tails back at him. He liked this so much that he kept coming back to the temple time and time again to meet up with his new friends.

I'm sure that you have experienced the truth of this story yourself. A positive attitude gets positive results; a negative attitude can end in failure or even disaster. Luckily, most of us don't break our neck as a consequence of being negative about ourselves and about life. However, it has been shown that you are more likely to fall ill and contract diseases like ulcers and even cancer when you think negatively a lot of the time. It appears that a negative attitude has an adverse effect on your immune system and also prevents wounds from healing quickly.

In 1987, tests were carried out at St Thomas's Hospital in London where a group of patients were played a tape with positive messages during their hysterectomy operation, sug-gesting to them that they would recover quickly and easily from their operation and that they would not experience any pain. When the test group was later compared to a control group who had undergone the same type of operation without hearing the positive messages, it was found that the patients of the test group recovered quicker and with less complications than the control group. The results were so impressive that they were even considered worthy of a note in The Lancet!

Positive thinking is also essential when you want to over-come your fear. In a way, buying this book has already been an act of positive thinking, hasn't it? You were saying to yourself, 'I'll get this book because it may show me a way out of my problem.' This thought shows that you concede that a solution might exist, so you are, albeit cautiously, optimistic, and why not?

Think back over the past years and remember other diffi-culties that have occurred in your life and how you managed to overcome those. Think about past achievements. They did not all just fall into your lap, did they? Some of the problems seemed impossible to sort out at the time, and you may have doubted that the mess could be disentangled or that you could find a way out of that particular difficulty, and yet you did.

Do you remember when you learnt to write? It seemed impossible to tell a 'p' from a 'q' — they looked so alike! You probably wondered how you would ever be able to tell them apart, until one day, after having tried for a while, you could do it.

Why is it that whenever we are faced with a new problem, we act as if it was the first one? We act as if past successes never happened; we don't believe in our abilities but instead worry a lot, rather than concentrating on finding a solution.

Many people feel a failure because of their fear. They feel inferior because their fear makes them different from others; it sets them apart because it disables them. Lots of people will not seek help because they feel ashamed that they have the fear in the first place. Please be aware that *the fear is not your fault*. As you have seen in Part I of the book, fears can come about for a variety of reasons, and practically all of them are external and can therefore not have been created by you or through your fault.

Your basic personality structure is there from the day you are born; you could not choose whether you were to be outgoing or shy. You also could not choose your parents, you could not choose the circumstances you grew up in, you could not choose whether your parents were caring or cruel. It is not your fault if you were humiliated or ignored and if, as a consequence, your confidence became low and you developed a fear-related problem. The notion that you are paying for inadequacies or sins in a previous life (karma) by experiencing problems in your present life, is, to me, a very negative concept, and smacks of the old Christian principle that you are automatically guilty the moment you are born.

We *all* make mistakes, we *all* do or have done things in the past which were wrong or hurtful to others. We *all* have to work on ourselves to be the best possible person we can be, but I strongly dispute that there is a God up there who sits and waits to punish us for mistakes we have made in the past. Some of us may be luckier than others in that our circumstances may be more favourable or that we have a more optimistic personality, and yet we can all be stricken by a fear problem in our life.

But equally, we all have the opportunity to get rid of that fear, provided we take responsibility for finding a solution and provided we are prepared to put some effort into our endeavours.

In this context, let me say very clearly that *it is possible to rid yourself of any fear as long as you are determined to work on it.* As you are reading this sentence you may think that you are the only exception, but let me assure you that there have been lots of people who have been to see me at my practice and thought like you, feeling that they were beyond help, and yet they got rid of their fear or anxiety. There is no way you can fail if only you persist, either on your own or with outside help.

Keep an open mind. Even though you may have no idea *how* you can make your fear disappear, believe that it is possible. Just because you can't see a way doesn't mean there is no way. If you can't believe in a solution, at least pretend that there is one. The more time you spend thinking about the successful outcome of your endeavours, the more motivated you feel to work on your fear problem and the more likely it is that you will solve it successfully (see also Vera Peiffer, *Positive Thinking*).

You will have to put effort into solving your fear problem, there is no doubt about that. When you employ some positive thinking strategies at the same time, you are going to have a better time while you are ploughing your way through to your aim, and why have a miserable time when you can have a good one?

Here are a few positive techniques to choose from.

Do more of what already works

When you wrote your diary, I asked you to watch out for any coping strategies that you find yourself employing. This is an important point because you could already have a solution there without knowing it.

Joan had suffered from anxiety for the last few years ever since she had taken her ageing father into her house. By keeping a diary, Joan discovered that her anxiety was worst when she disagreed with her father over something. Joan's father was not an easy person to live with, and besides, Joan had been used to having her own space ever since her husband died eight years ago.

The atmosphere between Joan and her father was quite tense, even though there were no direct arguments. Her father was still amazingly fit for his age but would not lift a finger to help Joan with any little chores in the house. Joan would come home from a long day's work to find that her father had not even bothered to take his breakfast cup and plate back to the kitchen.

Joan was aware that her father had been living like that for many years, with her mother waiting on him hand and foot. But even though she could intellectually *understand* all this, her emotions told her a very different story. She resented the fact that he would sit at home all day long, read magazines and watch television and not make any contribution towards looking after the household, when she was rushing around to accommodate his wishes in every way and deal with a demanding full-time job at the same time.

The one time she found her anxiety totally gone was when she lost her self-control and shouted at her father over something. She felt much better for a few hours afterwards, but then started feeling guilty that she had had a go at the old man. Still, it was quite a revelation to her that her outburst had got rid of the anxiety for a while. She was obviously onto something that worked, although she didn't much like to think that she had to be rude to her father in order to get rid of her anxiety. So how could she adapt her coping strategy to something more acceptable?

We sat down and decided that she needed to say something *before* she reached the point of no return. She needed to ask her father openly to help with a few simple tasks around the house while she was away. To her surprise, he reacted quite positively to her request which she had managed to put calmly and politely, and he started helping her around the house. He still remained a difficult man, but as Joan learnt to express her needs rather than supress them, things became a lot easier for her. Her anxiety disappeared and her relationship with her father improved, so everyone gained from her new strategy.

Look at your own diary. Are you already using something that works well for you? Maybe you find that doing work in your garden makes you feel better. Throw yourself into it! You may not only get rid of your anxiety but also win a prize for the best kept garden in the neighbourhood! Maybe you find that surrounding yourself with people makes you feel calmer. Send out those invitations *now*! Or the contrary may be the case – you are less anxious when you have a bit of peace and quiet. Make that space for yourself. Tell others that you do not want to be disturbed for an hour or two. Remove yourself from your environment if need be, go for a walk, go into town, buy yourself a magazine and have a cup of tea in a café. Whatever it is that works for you, do more of it. You have unwittingly found a solution to your problem, now go and use it to its fullest extent.

Spend time thinking about the positive outcome

You may decide to just use one of the solutions outlined in this chapter, or you may want to use a combination of several of them. It is a matter of personal preference which method or methods you choose and how you combine them.

While you are working with the various techniques, set a little time aside every day to 'daydream' about the time when you have achieved your aim, when you are free of your fear.

If you have a phobia about eating in public, imagine what it would be like to happily accept invitations to go out, to enjoy the food in the restaurant and have an interesting conversation at the same time. If you suffer from anxiety, picture in your mind how you wake up in the morning, feeling refreshed and ready to go, breezing through your day, feeling light and free. I know this sounds like cloud-cuckoo-land while you still have your fear, but it is possible to achieve this aim. Believe it, and if you can't, pretend that you believe it and daydream anyway. Other people have done it – you can do it too!

Indulge in these positive thoughts several times a day and also try to imagine the feelings that go with having achieved your aim, the sense of relief and freedom, the sense of pride in your ability to overcome adversity, the exhilaration of success. The more strongly you can feel those positive feelings, the more strongly you motivate yourself to go for that aim.

Whatever the mind can perceive, the mind can achieve; watch it happen!

You can take this positive thinking exercise even further by imagining that you are projected forward to a point where you have long overcome your fear. Imagine sitting in a time machine that takes you forward and sets you down at a time when your problems lay far behind you, and as you find yourself at that point in your life, look back into the past and contemplate those bad old days when you still used to suffer from that fear, and how you can't understand now how you could ever let yourself get so depressed over it as you did then. Watch as you are looking back in time how you got yourself out of that hole, how you worked on it and slowly progressed towards the point where you are now. Also, watch in your mind's eye your first break-through, 'remember' the first time that the fear was no longer ruling your life, and reminisce what a big event it was then and how it has now become such a common way of life for you to be free of that fear.

Thinking these types of thought repeatedly will impress a positive attitude on your subconscious mind, overriding the previous negative messages that kept coming to the conscious surface whenever you thought about doing something about your fear. Whatever you spend a lot of time thinking about will eventually come true, so instead of thinking about your fear, think about having overcome it. The secret is to persist in thinking positively, no matter what is happening around you, and as you are systematically changing your thought patterns to positive, you push yourself closer to your aim of being the happy and fearless person you want and deserve to be.

Use positive affirmations

Another useful technique in this context is to repeat certain key phrases to yourself. These are easy to remember because they are only short sentences. Write your favourite affirmations on pieces of paper and stick them onto surfaces around the house which you pass frequently – the fridge door, the mirror in the hall, the door of your wardrobe, the front door (from the *inside*, unless you think your neighbours and the milkman could do with a bit of positive thinking too). In addition, keep repeating these sentences to yourself while you are waiting for the bus or when you are out for a walk or when there is a lull at work.

Here are some suggestions for various fear problems. Select what appeals to you. If it feels right, it is right for you.

Agoraphobia

- I have conquered the inside of my house, I can conquer the outside too.
- I move easily and effortlessly past my boundaries.
- I am strong enough to push back the barricades that hold me in.
- Bit by bit I advance, safely and securely.

Panic attacks

- A panic attack may be unpleasant, but it cannot harm me.
- I am taking control again, in my own time, at my own pace.
- Nothing is forever, not even panic attacks.

Worrying

- I don't have time to worry about this now. I will worry about it later.
- I forget to worry more and more often.
- I have more important things to do than worry.

Phobia

- I don't want my phobia any more and I'm throwing it out now.
- The phobia is going, it just doesn't know it yet.

Exam/test nerves

- My concentration is so good during my exam/test that I find it quite easy.
- I surprise myself at how calm I am when it counts.
- Exams/tests are amazingly straightforward.

Social phobias

- I feel friendly towards others, and others feel friendly towards me.
- I mingle easily and effortlessly with others.
- Others accept me even though I overlook this fact sometimes.
- My confidence increases slowly but surely.

Watch your language

This is only a minor point, but nevertheless important. Whenever you speak to anyone about your phobia, tone down your vocabulary and even out the tone of your voice. Don't wave your arms about and exclaim at the top of your voice, 'I absolutely *hate* bridges! It makes me positively sick if I even get *near* one! I could *never ever* cross one even if you *paid* me!' Instead, keep your voice down, cut the information down to the bare essentials ('Bridges worry me. I don't like crossing them.') and take any exaggerated emotion out of your voice as far as possible.

Equally, don't whisper in a mousy little voice about how you turned into a nervous wreck last time you had to do a presentation at work. Speak normally and in a matter of fact way, for example, 'I felt very uncomfortable speaking in front of my colleagues, and I feel that I didn't really do myself justice.'

The more melodrama there is in your voice, the more you propel yourself into a frantic state of mind and keep on building up the problem in your mind. Put your fear onto your mental shopping list and treat it like any other 'To Do' item – something that is a bit of a chore but still needs to be dealt with.

Whenever you talk about your fear, it is not just other people who are listening, but also your own subconscious mind. Just as you can influence your subconscious with positive affirmations and images, you can also imprint negative messages on it, so keep a tab on how you speak about your fear problem.

The only place where this rule is unimportant is when you see a therapist who asks you in detail about your fear. In this case, it is appropriate to describe matters comprehensively, without worrying too much about what emotional components come across at the time.

PARADOXICAL INTENTION AND DEREFLECTION
Self-help and therapy
For social phobias, panic attacks and sexual problems

These are two very effective methods which were first used in 1929 by the Viennese psychiatrist Viktor E. Frankl who devised a psychological concept called Logotherapy which is concerned with man's fundamental search for meaning. Just like the behaviourist school of thought and many later forms of therapy, Frankl believed that it is not always necessary to look at the underlying cause to solve a fear problem.

It has long been a well-established fact that, in a phobia for example, it is the expectation of a recurrence of the fear that makes a relapse more likely. When your hand shakes as you pick up your cup of coffee in the presence of other people, you may well get into a pattern of expecting your hand to shake every time you pick up a cup in public. Because you are expecting it, you tense up, and as a consequence, your hand shakes again next time. Because your fearful expectations have proved correct, you are more and more convinced that you have a problem, and your attention becomes very focused on this particular area. Wherever you go, you are always *aware* that your hands tremble and you start avoiding having to pick up a cup when others are around. At the same time you find that you are perfectly capable of holding a cup steadily when you are on your own. But no matter how hard you try, you cannot hold your hand steady when other people are there with you.

When using paradoxical intention, the therapist will encourage the client to reverse their intention. Instead of trying to stop the shaking, the therapist will challenge the client *to shake intentionally*, to shake as fast as possible and to spill as much of the drink as they can; in others words, paradoxical intention means *prescribing* the symptom rather than trying to make it go away.

Initially, this can appear to be an illogical request to make of the client, but the results soon justify the means. Just as it is true to say that the harder you try to stop shaking the less you can do it, it is equally true to say that the harder you try to shake the less you can do it. As the client is urged to produce his symptom on purpose, he faces his fear at the same time. In other words, he begins to control his fear rather than the fear controlling him. This way, the vicious circle of self-fulfilling prophecy is disrupted, the client feels in control, more relaxed and can therefore stop being afraid of shaking, and this will actually stop him shaking.

In many cases, paradoxical intention works immediately after applying it only once. A friend of mine had a massive panic attack at noon one day. There was no apparent reason for it, and it seemed to come completely out of the blue. As anyone who has ever had a panic attack knows, it is quite a horrifying experience, and it is not surprising that you would worry about it recurring again, and my friend certainly did.

However, she decided not to be defeated by this. When 12 o'clock drew near on the next day she told herself, 'OK, let's do this properly. If I'm going to have another panic attack, I might as well record it!' and she switched on her tape recorder. She did not have another panic attack.

In using paradoxical intention, you can either use thoughts, speak those thoughts out loud or use a written script as I do with my clients. Here is an example.

Geraldine came to see me because she was afraid of having a panic attack while waiting at the bus stop. This fear went back to the time she had had severe period pains while waiting at the bus stop, feeling weak and afraid she might faint. She had to hold on to a rail to steady herself so as not to fall. When the bus finally arrived, she was shaking all over and collapsed into a seat. Ever since then she felt in a high state of anxiety at the bus stop, especially if the bus was a long time. She was so concerned about her fear that she would have avoided going on the bus if it hadn't been too far to walk to work and home.

First of all, I discussed with Geraldine what she considered to be the worst thing that could possibly happen to her if she had another panic attack at the bus stop. She thought about it and replied that it would probably be if she fell to the ground and people saw her lying there, out of control, and the feeling of embarrassment and humiliation that would go with such a situation.

Once we had established what Geraldine's expectations were I wrote her the following note:

> Today is the biggest day of my life. Today I'm going to show everyone! I'm determined to have the panic attack of my life. No more half measures from now on – I'll make it a good one this time. I've decided that I'm going to drop to the ground and foam from the mouth. I'll scream and shout and everybody will look at me. I just hope that the bus is really late so I have more time to work myself up for my great performance. I'm going to cause a real scene, and the more people see it, the better. And tomorrow it is going to be in all the newspapers!

I asked Geraldine to read out the note aloud to me, with emphasis. She did and started laughing, saying she didn't think she could actually do all this dropping down and foaming from the mouth, so I told her that all I wanted her to do was read the note over and over again as she was standing at the bus stop and try and do her best.

Geraldine was not at all convinced by her task but neverthe-less promised to carry it out conscientiously. In the evening I had a telephone call from her saying she could not believe what had happened. She had kept reading the note, and even though the bus was quite late in arriving, she had felt calm and collected and had had a perfectly pleasant journey home even though she didn't get a seat, which would normally have worried her.

In another instance, a young man came to see me. He was engaged to be married but felt he couldn't go ahead with the marriage because of his problem of being unable to eat in public places with a woman. This meant that he could never take his fiancée out to a restaurant or go on holiday with her unless it was self-catering.

The first occurrence of his phobia happened when he had been out for lunch with two girls from the office. They all had pizza and were chatting when he started to feel extremely ill and had to excuse himself, went to the toilet and was sick. Even though the girls were very sympathetic and nice about the incident, he had felt profoundly embarrassed and inconsolable that such a thing should have happened to him.

From that time on, he avoided eating in public and even became anxious about eating at his fiancée's place. He always made sure that he hadn't eaten for at least six hours before he went to see her so that his stomach was totally empty and there was no danger of him being sick in her presence.

We carefully looked at the original event to check whether there was any discernible reason why he should have felt sick. He recalled under hypnosis the conversation they had had on the day, but there was nothing there that seemed to have upset him. We looked at the possibility that his phobia might have been a way of avoiding marriage, but again, the results were negative. He did not respond sufficiently well to gradual desensitization and we did not seem to get anywhere with the problem. At this stage, paradoxical intention seemed the last resort.

I suggested to my client that there was a method which worked very well, but that it was rather strange and I wasn't sure whether he would be prepared to try it out. My client assured me however that he would try out *anything* if it would get rid of his problem. I then told him that if he could, only *once*, be sick on purpose in a restaurant while his girlfriend was with him, he'd be rid of the problem.

He was visibly taken aback by the idea of having to go and do this, but he was willing to give it a go. He wanted to know whether he had to be sick at the table or would it count if he was sick in the toilet? I told him that I'd prefer him to be sick at the table if he could, and he finally went off, promising to do his best.

He came back a week later, not very pleased with himself. He reported that he had been to a restaurant with his girlfriend and that he had been extremely nervous. They had ordered food and he had eaten some of it and, indeed, felt quite sick, but hadn't actually managed to throw up. He showed with his hand how the feeling of sickness had come up to the middle of his chest, but he hadn't succeeded in bringing it up any higher so that he could vomit.

I shook my head in disappointment and told him sternly that this wasn't really good enough and to go away and try harder next week.

When he came back the following week he was totally dejected. His first words were, 'It isn't me! I've tried everything!' And he continued to report that he had been to a restaurant with his girlfriend on a Saturday when it was particularly crowded (a day which he dreaded most), had sat right in the middle of the restaurant (last time he had sat on the side, near the doors to the toilets), had ordered everything on the menu, even those things that he disliked, ate it all, but had been unable to be sick. 'Even worse,' he added morosely, 'after a while I even started relaxing!' But he was determined to fulfil his task, so he went down to the toilet and stuck his finger down his throat — and he still couldn't be sick! He confessed to having failed miserably, but not for lack of trying.

At this point, I reminded him of the reason why he had come to me in the first place. We established that the reason had been that he couldn't eat in a public place when a woman was present, but that he had done just that last week. Since he had to admit that he had really done absolutely everything to be sick but failed, surely he didn't stand a chance of ever being sick if he went into a restaurant and *didn't even try* to be sick! His face lit up as he realized that his problem was indeed solved and he went off a happy man.

Paradoxical intention is equally useful as a self-help programme. In this context it is irrelevant that you know how the 'trick' works — it works anyway. Most people who use it on themselves find it easiest to write a note which they read again and again.

When you write yourself such a note, make sure you phrase the sentences clearly as *intentions*. Use expressions like 'I am determined' or 'I have decided' and express clearly your aim of making this into a big thing. Areas where you will find paradoxical intention useful are facial ticks, insomnia ('I am determined to stay awake, come what may!'), worrying, panic attacks, and it even works when you apply it to tiresome habits your kids might develop — instead of blowing your top because your four-year-old keeps running around the table instead of eating her food, tell her to run a lot faster. Chances are she is going to sit down because she is not going to give you the satisfaction of getting things your way . . .

The second method which Frankl developed is dereflection. He had been using this method since the 1940s, and it was later extended and refined by Masters and Johnson in 1970. Here, the aim is to distract the client's attention from their own problem and focus their interest onto something else so they can stop thinking about their problem and thereby reinstate spontaneous behaviour. This is a technique which is of great benefit in cases where a person does too much thinking and is consequently incapable of relaxing, for example in sexual matters.

In a sexually liberated age where contraception has become readily available and where there is a growing number of single people in society, there is a lot more pressure on men and women to 'do it'. Having sex is, in spite of AIDS, still very much an 'in' thing to do, and just now we see more and more articles about not just one orgasm but multiple ones! For quite a while, it has been claimed that women should be capable of several orgasms during intercourse, but now that wave is reaching out to men.

Increased media focus on sex and continuous sexual innuendos in advertising draw attention to the fact that being sexy is a must if you want to be successful, and this creates growing pressure to perform for both men and women. This is of course bad news for an activity that depends on a relaxed and spontaneous approach. Vaginism, frigidity and impotence are all problems that come from wanting to do well but being afraid at the same time. When you are trying too hard to perform something which will only function spontaneously, you are unlikely to succeed. But how to be spontaneous on purpose?

Therapists will usually help their clients achieve this aim by instructing the client to do something which takes their attention away from their sexual problem. A woman who is incapable of experiencing an orgasm might be asked to pay a lot of attention to her partner. A couple where the man is impotent will be asked to spend every evening in bed and concentrate on foreplay only, with strict instructions to avoid penetration. As the focus is now on foreplay, pressure is taken away from penetration, so that an erection can happen spontaneously and successful intercourse can take place eventually.

Dereflection is also a useful aid in cases where a woman cannot conceive because of emotional tension. If there are problems conceiving, this can be a consequence of being too intense and getting too wound up over the issue so that the body tenses up and is less and less able to work normally and to conceive easily. This type of infertility is often solved spontaneously once the couple have taken time off and gone on holiday where they can relax and start thinking about other things. In other cases, conception happened when the couple had given up all hope and adopted a child – the pressure was off, the woman relaxed and conceived!

Another area where dereflection can help is in sports. If a certain motion has been practised sufficiently, for example serving the ball in tennis, an overambitious player can easily ruin his or her serve by trying too hard to get it right, thereby interfering with the natural flow of movement. In order to restore this natural flow, the player needs to focus his or her attention on, for example, the upward movement of the arm that throws the ball so that attention is taken away from the arm which is holding the racket. That way, the racket-arm can perform the correct sequence of movements in an uninhibited manner.

Paradoxical intention and dereflection are particularly useful for people who tend to try too hard to get things right, for those who find it difficult to relax and for those who have problems resolving fears that have become a habit.

HYPNO-ANALYSIS
Therapy
For simple phobias, social phobias, fear of performance, anxiety and panic attacks

This form of therapy has become more widely used over the last ten years for conditions such as anxiety, panic attacks and various phobias, especially those where the origin is unknown.

Freud himself initially used hypnosis as a tool to discover underlying causes for his patients' neurotic symptoms, but gave it up because he assumed that hypno-analysis was getting unreliable results when several of his female patients started revealing memories of incest under hypnosis. The concept of sexual abuse within the family, however, was so unacceptable to Freud's nineteenth-century mind that he dismissed his patients' incest memories as wishful thinking, stating that they must be founded on unconscious sexual urges the women felt towards their father.

Hypno-analysis combines a psychoanalytical process with the use of hypnosis. Whereas other forms of therapy such as Neuro-linguistic programming (NLP), desensitization and positive thinking deal with the *symptom*, hypno-analysis tackles the problem from a different angle by looking for the root of the problem. The theory behind this approach is that no problem occurs without a cause. No child is born with a phobia or with panic attacks. When we enter this world, we are equipped with a vast supply of confidence, and it is only when negative or detrimental experiences occur that we lose this confidence and become anxious or phobic. It is therefore necessary, according to hypno-analysis, to look at those negative experiences and work through them so that the sufferer can be free of the emotional stresses that these past events have created. Once the past has been sorted out, the tension goes and with it the anxiety or the panic attacks.

Tension can build up over many years, and when it gets too much, you either explode or implode. Explosions happen in the form of temper tantrums or panic attacks; implosions result in depressions and nervous breakdowns which occur when the body is unable to contain the mounting pressures any longer and collapses. If you have had a rough time as a child, with parents who were violent or absent a lot or where the parents didn't take an interest in you, or if you come from a background where you were repeatedly put down or ridiculed, then this can result in low self-confidence and feelings of helplessness and vulnerability – ideal breeding ground for anxiety! If you then go on to marry someone who is negative or discouraging, the tension starts building up even more. Any further problems like grievances at work or complications in your family life can be all that is needed to trigger off the first panic attack or plunge you into a state of near-permanent anxiety.

Tension is usually generated by a number of events in the past or by one or two high impact occurrences. Frequent conflict between parents can make a child fearful, as can one grave accident or one single occurrence of physical abuse. If you have ever had the bad luck to be physically attacked unexpectedly, you will know how you remain fearful for months, sometimes for years afterwards, dreading that the same thing might happen again. Men and women who have been fighting in a war or who have been held hostage often find that they are haunted by nightmarish memories of the past that will not allow them to sleep soundly or to live a life unrestricted by fear.

If you find that you compulsively mull over miserable childhood memories or past failures, coupled with a feeling of guilt, and if you suffer from a fear problem today, you will find hypno-analysis a powerful and effective tool to unravel and remove the causes of your fear.

Having worked with hypno-analysis for years, I am aware that many people are initially concerned about this type of therapy. They are worried that they might open a can of worms or that they may be unable to cope once they have uncovered the cause. To some people, it appears safer to live with the well-known enemy of anxiety, rather than to set out into the land of potentially upsetting memories. This is of course a choice everyone has to make for themselves. The fact, however, is that it may be uncomfortable and unsettling to go through analysis, but most people find that it is only half as bad as they thought it would be. Once the skeleton is out of the cupboard it loses its power over you. Also, your therapist will not leave you in the lurch the moment you find the underlying cause. He or she will immediately help you to work through the traumatic memory so that you can come to terms with it emotionally and then let go of it.

The reason why hypnosis is used in this context is that it makes it easier to access memories. Hypnosis is a state of gentle relaxation and concentration where you are perfectly capable of hearing and remembering everything that is being said to you and where you yourself can speak and remember quite easily.

Rather than being unconscious, your awareness is heightened, which in turn enables you to remember more easily and therefore cuts down on the number of sessions you need to resolve the problem. The hypno-analytical process usually takes between six and twelve sessions.

In some cases, for example with many phobias, there is a direct and obvious link between the original event and the consequent phobia. If you have been stung by a bee once, you may develop a phobia for bees and similar insects. When, however, the fear is no longer a direct translation of the underlying cause, as is the case with panic attacks for example, the sufferer is usually at a loss how to explain it.

Picture the following scene. You are in the supermarket, about to do your shopping. There is nothing in particular that is worrying you right now. You are just reaching for a packet of cornflakes when it happens. It is like an iron claw gripping your heart; your chest is tightening up, you are rooted to the spot, you find it impossible to move, your heart is racing and you can feel cold sweat breaking out all over your body. You may even feel like fainting so that you have to sit or lie down. Should you be taken to hospital as a consequence, they will automatically check whether you have had a heart attack. They will find that there is nothing wrong with your heart and send you home, telling you that it was nothing or that you suffer from stress or anxiety. At this point, advice normally ranges from pulling yourself together to the recommendation to go and see a psychiatrist. What you should be told at this point is that you have experienced a panic attack and that, rather than popping pills, you will have to have a closer look at your life in order to get rid of them.

And even when a panic attack is not severe enough to land you in hospital, it is still a horrendous experience. Because it descends on you out of the blue, many sufferers feel that they are going mad. They don't know *when* it is going to hit them, *where* it is going to happen and how bad it is going to be this time. It is like a secret, vicious enemy that stalks you, and however much you try to brace yourself, you are never quite prepared when it strikes again. It is a feeling of having absolutely no control over what is happening to you, and it is this feeling which gives you the first clue to what the underlying cause is.

In the following, I will give you two case histories of clients who came to see me with a fear problem and had a successful resolution of the problem through hypno-analysis.

Eva had been suffering from severe panic attacks for the last eight years, ever since her marriage to Tony. Her mother had not approved of Eva marrying and had told her on the day she went away that she was sending her old mother to an early grave by deserting her like that. Up to this point, Eva had always been the dutiful daughter, as opposed to her sister Elizabeth who would talk back and generally be a lot less obliging than Eva. But despite her obedient and considerate behaviour, Eva could never get it right for her mother. If she made the beds, the mother would come along and remake them; if she cleaned the kitchen floor, the mother would give it an extra wipe afterwards. Even later, when Eva was married and her mother came to stay (surprisingly, she hadn't died after all!), the mother would go on about how fabulous a cook Elizabeth was, without as much as mentioning the quality of Eva's cooking.

Eva's husband Tony didn't help either. He would not lift a finger at home, leaving everything including decorating and painting to Eva who, just like Tony, had a full-time job *and* their little boy Carlo to look after.

Tony's family were first generation Italians who would gossip about absent family members in great detail during their family get-togethers. They would also criticize a lot, and it was especially those who were a bit shy who had to bear the brunt. Whenever Eva and her family went to visit at her aunt's, the aunt would comment on Eva's husband and son being so thin and enquire whether Eva was feeding her men properly. When Carlo was born, Eva's mother-in-law stayed in hospital with Eva for a week and would not allow Eva to have the baby near her, insisting on keeping the cot away from Eva's bedside. Whenever Eva was holding the baby, the mother-in-law would come along and take it from her. Eva, who had had a Caesarian, was desperate to get to know her baby, but being afraid of offending her mother-in-law, didn't say anything. At the same time, she got very agitated and angry until she finally burst into tears and told her mother-in-law to let her have her baby.

In the following years, there were many more occasions where relatives took over Eva's life, and she started feeling more and more out of control. She was angry at what was happening, but she did not have the courage to say anything. In the end, she was so wound up that even just *thinking* about her relations made her feel tense and uncomfortable.

At work it was the same. She would never say anything when colleagues were not pulling their weight or when they did something that upset her. And then, of course, there were the panic attacks on top of everything. She felt anxious all the time anyway — that had become quite normal. But when the panic attacks struck, she felt so bad afterwards that she had to leave the room, no matter where she was, and she would break down and cry in desperation. At times she was so low that she even thought of committing suicide.

What was happening here was that Eva was desperately trying to keep the lid of good manners on her anger about the interfering treatment she received from her family and relatives. But every once in a while, the accumulated anger would become stronger than, symbolically speaking, the arm that was holding down the lid, and she would 'explode' via a panic attack. Her body was making sure that it relieved the tension every once in a while by venting the suppressed emotions via a panic attack, since the normal channel of having a massive row with the relatives was blocked by Eva's refusal to admit to her anger. She had been brought up to be a 'nice' girl, a dutiful daughter and daughter-in-law, listening to the advice her elders gave her. And even though these elders put her down most of the time, she found it difficult to acknowledge these facts. She would even defend her difficult aunt, saying the aunt had 'always been like that' and really, deep down, she had a 'heart of gold'.

As therapy progressed, the connection between Eva's anger and the panic attacks became clearer. The worst attacks would always occur when she was expecting to see her relatives or when something at the office had annoyed her for a while. Step by step, Eva learnt to express her feelings in a constructive manner. She began to sort out the events that had caused her problems in the past, and she also learnt to stand up for herself, both at home and at work. As her confidence increased, her relations became a lot less bossy with her; she even was given compliments for her cooking by her mother now!

For the first time, she began to feel in control of her life, and whenever something annoyed her, she sorted it out on the spot, so there was no chance for her anger to build up in the way that it had done before. Her relations are much more respectful these days, and rather than forcing their advice on her, they now ask Eva for her advice. Eva's panic attacks have now become a thing of the past.

You can see in this example how powerful feelings can become when they get repressed. Eva had done such a superb (subconscious) job of stashing away her anger that she had practically forgotten that it was there. It was only when the anger had built up to an unbearable level and started 'exploding' in the form of panic attacks that she sought help and finally got in touch with her perfectly justified feelings of anger. Once that had happened she could start to use her anger productively and thus take control of her life again.

The second case history is that of Jennifer. She came with a fear of injections that was so extreme that she was unable to allow anyone to take a blood sample or give her a jab or even go for electrolysis to have hair on her legs removed.

This phobia had not been a real problem until she and her husband decided that they wanted to start a family. Jennifer knew that when she got pregnant she would have to have blood taken, and apart from that she did not want to pass on her phobia to her children. She had been very brave on previous occasions, trying to master her fear. Several times she got as far as sitting in her GP's office, but when the nurse came up to her with the needle, she went hysterical and could not go through with it.

This fear of injections seemed to date back to her teenage years but not before then. She could remember one incident before the age of ten when she had been perfectly all right when given an injection.

Jennifer came from a large family with six children. She grew up with a stepfather, her own father having died in an accident when she was three. The same accident had left her mother very ill so that the family was in constant worry over the mother's health.

Even though her memory was very good, some of her teenage years remained a mystery to Jennifer. She had no recollections of her life between the age of twelve and fifteen. She could not recall any specific memories during that time at all. (This was a piece of significant information for me, as a blanked out time span is usually a sign that there is repressed material hidden away in it.)

Once Jennifer had learnt to go into hypnosis, we began to trace her fear back into the past. As she described in hypnosis all the feelings that were associated with her phobia, I asked her to go back in time and find a memory that was linked to similar feelings. She remembered various incidents in doctor's surgeries where she had experienced the same feelings of panic when she was about to be injected, but when we got to her teenage years, a very different memory started emerging. She began to remember vaguely an unpleasant and frightening incident to do with two men, and somehow that memory seemed linked to a feeling of alarm and pain.

Throughout the next sessions, the memory gradually became clearer, and with it, strong feelings of guilt emerged. It turned out that Jennifer had been going out with a girlfriend, Kate, who came from a home where the parents were not getting on and the children were left to their own devices. As a consequence, Kate was drifting in and out of cafés and seemed incredibly streetwise to the thirteen-year-old Jennifer who admired her and was happy to tag along. Kate drank alcohol and seemed to know quite a number of young men.

One day, Kate suggested that they go and buy a bottle of vodka. Jennifer, once again impressed by her friend's audacity, agreed and the girls went into an off-licence where they were sold the vodka without any problems. The girls wandered about for a while and finally ended up in a café which was one of Kate's haunts. They ordered sandwiches and, every once in a while, took surreptitious swigs from the bottle which they kept hidden under the table. Jennifer had never had any alcohol before but was quite willing to try to show that she could hold her own. The vodka didn't taste very strong, but soon both girls started feeling a bit dizzy.

In the meantime, they had been joined by two young men whom Kate seemed to know. The men sat down at their table and started chatting to them. By now, Jennifer was feeling very unwell and Kate, who also started feeling drunk, suggested going back to her parents', knowing that they were not at home. They left the café together, and as soon as she was out in the fresh air, Jennifer felt so sick that she vomited. She felt shaky and dazed from the alcohol and did not want to go back to Kate's place with the others but was overruled. She felt physically too weak to put up much of a resistance.

Meanwhile, the two young men had stopped a cab, and before Jennifer could protest, they were on their way.

During the taxi ride, both men started touching up the girls. Jennifer, who still felt violently sick and distressed, tried to fend off the advances, but to no avail. The taxi driver noticed what was going on in the back of his cab but did not say or do anything.

Somehow they all got up into Kate's flat, and the next thing Jennifer remembered was being pinned down and feeling that she was ripped apart and in intense pain, and these feelings seemed to go on forever. She also remembered stinging pains on her arms *as if someone was jabbing needles into her*. In one of the later sessions we found out what really happened – apparently the two men had put out their cigarettes on her arms after they had both raped her, and then left her lying on the floor, bleeding, with her clothes torn off.

She didn't feel she could tell anyone, least of all her sick mother, for fear that the shock might kill her. She also felt that she had brought the entire misery onto herself. It was all her own fault – she should not have drunk the alcohol, and she should not have consented to go along to Kate's flat.

All this information emerged gradually as the memories started coming back under hypnosis, accompanied by strong feelings of guilt and self-accusations. We had now found the reason why she was afraid of injections. They reminded her of her awful experience when she was thirteen when the burning cigarettes stung her arms and felt like injections.

It is true to say that we cannot change what has happened in the past, but we can certainly change the way we *feel* about what happened. For Jennifer, it was now a matter of setting the record straight and putting the events into perspective. This was an important further step for her to work through because, after all, Jennifer was still feeling helpless and vulnerable whenever she thought or talked about the rape. These feelings needed to be turned around into more active emotions so that she could start feeling in control of her life again and, as a consequence, shed her fear of injections.

We started going over the events and looking at them from an outsider's point of view, starting with her trip to the off-licence. Under hypnosis, I asked Jennifer to have a good look at that memory by pretending she could see it as a film on a cinema screen. Once she was able to adopt an adult outsider's stance, she found that she felt quite annoyed at the man in the off-licence who sold alcohol to two obviously underage girls. She became aware of the fact that she and her friend were really only children who were experimenting, and that the real responsibility in this particular scene lay with the adult, that is the man in the off-licence who should have been responsible enough not to sell them the vodka.

We then proceeded to the scene in the café, again looking at it from an outsider's point of view. On looking at the memory on the cinema screen, Jennifer had to admit that she could not have realized at that age what effect the vodka would have on her, especially since she had never had any alcohol before. As an adult observer of the scene, she could see that the girls were doing something very silly, but at the same time she was aware that they could not possibly know that they were meddling with a substance that would make them sick. On the screen, Jennifer could acknowledge the event for what it was – two very young and immature girls getting themselves into trouble through ignorance.

Gradually, the powerful feelings of guilt were beginning to lift as we looked at the taxi ride and how the driver had been aware of what was happening but did not intervene. Jennifer felt angry at this, so I asked her to imagine herself going into the screen and expressing her annoyance to the cab driver, which she did.

Then came the hardest part where Jennifer had to look at the rape scene from the outside. By this stage, she felt a lot stronger already for having expressed her anger various times in previous sessions, so she was not too shaken by finally facing the last scene on the screen. She was quite clear that nobody could possibly have been asking for what was happening to the girl in the screen. In her mind, she went into the screen and did with the attackers what they had done to her and then beat them to pulp for good measure. She emerged from this session very relieved and very much happier than she had been in a long time.

The whole hypno-analysis took nine sessions after which Jennifer was capable of having electrolysis done on her legs, and a few weeks later she had an injection without any further problems.

In Jennifer's case, the cause for her fear was initially hidden away in her subconscious mind, which makes her case history look somewhat sensational. I must emphasize, however, that in most cases, the cause is much more mundane and often even consciously known to the client. The problem is often that the client does not realize how much this incident affected them at the time.

When we as adults look back on our childhood, we often tend to forget how different life is for children who cannot easily extricate themselves from hurtful or unbearable situations, simply because they don't have the power or the know-how to do so. Being bullied at school, for example, is not a minor matter. Think about it! Imagine you had to go to work every day and one of your colleagues would threaten to beat you up (and do it too) unless you gave him or her money. Consider the terror you would feel every morning, knowing that you will have to face that person again, wondering whether you will get away without getting physically threatened or not. As an adult, at least you would have the power to change jobs; a child does not have that luxury!

You are very vulnerable as a child. Rebukes weigh more heavily, humiliations cut deeper and failures hurt more and will leave more pronounced effects than they would on an adult.

Hypno-analysis is a powerful tool that can help resolve past trauma and reset the balance so that negative feelings can be linked with the memories that have occasioned them in the first place and then be left behind in the past where they belong.

FLOODING
Supervised self-help
For worrying, simple phobias and fear of performance

Flooding is a process whereby a person is, more or less suddenly, exposed to a situation that would normally arouse a high level of anxiety in them. In contrast to the technique of desensitization, flooding does not allow a gradual approach but requires a person to go into a fear-inducing situation more or less unprepared. The person is consequently forced, or forces themselves, to confront their fear head on and to its fullest extent; in other words, they are allowing the fear to totally engulf or 'flood' them.

As you can imagine, this can either work wonderfully well or go terribly wrong. To lock someone with a cat phobia into a room full of cats is, to say the least, totally irresponsible, and at worst can send that person into a heart attack or insanity. Throwing a child in at the deep end to teach it to swim is both cruel and ineffective. To force a youngster to fetch something from the basement when you know they are terrified to go there is inhuman because the child's fear does not diminish but, on the contrary, increases. The child's trust in the parent is severely shaken and its self-confidence weakened, and this in turn increases the fear even more. In addition, the child also feels guilty for being inadequate and is thus left with an emotional burden which may well hold it back in other aspects of its life.

So why have a whole section on this method if it is so harmful?

The fact is that this way of dealing with fear can be very successful if it is employed with your permission and supervised by a person who is experienced in dealing with this technique. Flooding can also be a successful self-help measure. It should, however, never be employed if you feel emotionally unstable or if you have had a problem with depression, anxiety or multiple phobias for a long time.

Certain personality types thrive on exposing themselves to danger on a regular basis. Stuntmen, boxers, mountaineers, cavers and performing artists need a high tolerance for fear. And yet, people who voluntarily seek these occupations do not necessarily have a higher fear threshold than the average person – on the contrary. Often, these are people who have been through trauma in the past or have had a tough time as a child. Even though they have come through it, they still have to prove to themselves (and others) that they are in control of their fear.

Facing and overcoming great fear on a professional basis can also have an addictive quality. People become turned on by the 'high' they get once the danger has been successfully overcome, and it is this euphoric feeling afterwards that they are recreating for themselves every time they face their fear again. In a way, one could almost speak of a secondary gain (see also p. 44) in these cases.

People who are basically emotionally stable and have chosen to expose themselves to a frightening situation and have successfully come through it speak of a feeling of enlightenment and greater understanding about themselves, as well as a fundamental strengthening of their character and their confidence in themselves.

In the course of writing this book, I came across one particularly interesting account which contains two cases of flooding within one experience. The lady who told me about this experience, Natasha, happened to mention the fact that she had spent a holiday in America during which she had learnt a great deal about the Native American Indian tradition. At the end of her visit, she and the group she was with embarked on a Vision Quest which turned out to be of great significance to each of the participants. This is Natasha's story.

The whole experience was part of a two-week trip to New Mexico. The Vision Quest itself actually took place on the very last weekend, so we had two weeks to acclimatize to the culture and climate. We went to Native American Indian museums, we saw the very colourful tribal ceremonies and visited the Indian villages. So by the time we got to the Vision Quest we had already had some experience of the Native American Indian tradition.

It's quite interesting looking back on it all now. At the time, I don't think I had really understood exactly what the Vision Quest was, or indeed the circumstances that were involved – I think that part of my mind shut it out; somehow, at a conscious level, I didn't really want to know because if I had realized exactly what was going to happen, I would probably have found an excuse not to put myself through the experience, and yet deep down I felt that there was something extremely important about it.

Natasha explained that the Vision Quest is an ancient tradition of the Native American Indian peoples. During a Vision Quest you spend some time alone and away from your familiar surroundings. Traditionally, this time is spent outside in a remote location such as a wood, forest or mountain, depending on where you live. Often a sense of harmony with the earth is felt and this is a time when the inner aspects of yourself come more into your consciousness as your focus on the outer world is reduced to a very simple level. This can be a very enriching experience.

There are increasing numbers of people today who can see the value and the benefit of going through this process which requires you to remove yourself from your normal circumstances and put yourself in a position where you are out in contact with nature, without any other human beings, so that you are totally on your own. Natasha continues:

The day before we were due to travel to our Vision Quest site, I experienced a situation in which I was able to face one of my fears head on. I was sitting near a river with a couple of other people and our Native American Indian guide. I happened to mention to him that I had a fear of coming face to face with a rattlesnake, and that I felt I would soon have to confront this fear in some way. He told me that it was unusual to see rattlesnakes in broad daylight and even if I did, I shouldn't worry about it. Well, I thought, it's all very well for you to say that, having grown up with rattlesnakes as a part of your life, but having never had the experience of seeing one, it was an awesome thought for me.

A little while later, we got up to leave. We hadn't walked more than a few paces when a little boy ran up from the river to where we had been sitting. Immediately he started shouting, 'Mum, come and look at this, there is a huge rattlesnake in the grass!' and sure enough, about four feet from where we had been sitting was an enormous rattlesnake lying quite still in the grass. Well, our guide suggested that this was the opportunity that I had been waiting for! I did feel afraid but I knew that I simply had to go and face that snake. Once I had done so, I felt an enormous sense of relief, as if a great weight had lifted from me. Although it may sound rather strange, I also felt grateful to the snake for coming to give me the opportunity to face my fear and then walk away from it.

This incident is an excellent example of voluntary flooding. Natasha was fully aware that she had this fear of rattlesnakes, and she expressed this fear openly to her guide. Even though he reassured her that it was unusual to see rattlesnakes in daylight, she was still doubtful as to whether she would be able to cope should she see one. And yet, when the unexpected opportunity to face the fear arose, Natasha did not spend too much time thinking about it but just went and did it. She instinctively did the right thing – had she hesitated for too long, she might have found it harder to face the snake, simply because she would have given herself too much time to build up fearful thoughts in her mind. Natasha continues:

We started our preparation for the Vision Quest by doing a 24-hour fast, the reason for this being that fasting cleanses and purifies the body, but it also sensitizes your nerves and your senses. We drove to the south of Colorado where we were to do the Vision Quest, to a large area of land which was mainly virgin territory with beautiful trees and a river running through it. It was a very long journey and we arrived there late in the afternoon. As the day wore on I began to realize more and more what I was actually letting myself in for. As the time drew nearer I became increasingly anxious about it and I was wondering whether I would have the courage to go through with this experience of spending a whole night on my own out in a forest in Colorado.

We finally arrived, later than we had anticipated. We were all led off into the forest and were each taken to our own Vision Quest site. We were simply shown where to stay and then left on our own after being told not to wander away from that site until someone came to fetch us at noon the next day.

It was quite a dense forest, with bushes on all four sides of the small area that was to be my 'home' for the next 20 hours or so. There were trees fallen down and bracken everywhere, and I couldn't see much beyond the immediate perimeter of my Vision Quest site. The only thing that showed that anyone had ever been in that part of the forest before were four red ribbons tied onto the trees and bushes, one for each quarter marking the north, south, east and west directions. We were not really given any instructions as to what we should actually *do* while we were there – I guess it was up to each of us to find that out for ourselves.

When my guide left me, I felt a very strong sense of panic; I was *really* afraid. At that point I felt like crying out, 'Hey, wait a minute, don't leave me here, I want to go back with you. I can't go through with this, it's too much!'. Once he was gone, however, I tried to gather myself together and thought, no, wait, sit down, you'll be OK, you'll deal with it somehow, it'll be all right. I had a sleeping bag and a coat with me because we had been told that it got extremely cold at night. I also had a tiny flashlight, a candle, pen and paper and a bottle of water to drink.

My first task was to get my sleeping bag out and put my things in order before it became too dark to see anything. That was also the first thing that I could think of to do to try to make myself feel less afraid and somehow more prepared for whatever ordeal the coming night would bring.

For the first hours, I was just totally full of fear of anything and everything that might happen. Nothing actually *did* happen, but every noise, every movement, every crackle of every twig made me jump and look to see if I could find out what, if anything, had made the noise in the first place. It took me a long time to realize that most of the sounds were simply the forest's own natural sounds. Many hours had to pass before I became acclimatized to my new environment.

I thought a great deal during that time and I wondered what my fear was all about, and where it came from. What exactly was I afraid of? It wasn't really fear of the darkness, because that's not something that bothers me too much; it was more a question of fear of the unknown. I felt I was out of my depth in such an unfamiliar environment that was full of wild creatures that might approach me. How would I deal with that if it happened? I also realized how small and insignificant I seemed in contrast to the vast and powerful forces of the earth and the creatures we share the earth with. So for the first few hours I went through all these thoughts and many more besides. At the same time I was trying to deal with the very real physical sensation of being almost too afraid to move, with my muscles really tensed up, ready to get up and run from some unknown fear at any time.

On my site there was a very tall tree that I was sitting against, and somehow I felt very comforted by the tree being there, and I was able to draw a lot of strength from that tree. Something else which really helped me was the beauty of the stars in the sky above me. There were so many stars and they were so bright — it was a very clear night and I must have seen at least half a dozen shooting stars that night; it was absolutely incredible. My mind kept switching from these sources of strength back to my fear, and then returning more frequently to the magnificence of the tree and the stars.

As time wore on, I realized that I had various options. Either I was going to spend the rest of the night filled with fear, with all my muscles tensed up and jumping at every sound, or I could stand up and scream and hope that somebody found me. Or I could just let go of my fear and start to relax and enjoy the beauty and peace of my surroundings. The more I thought about my fear, the more I realized that I wasn't actually afraid of anything specific that was happening there and then. I realized that I was afraid of what *might* happen at some point in the near future. But then again, it might not happen at all!

The more I realized that, the more I was able just to let go of the fear. I realized that if you live fully in the present moment, as in fact all ancient wisdom suggests you do, there is no fear, no fear at all. At that point, I really understood the meaning of the saying that the only thing to fear is fear itself, and that struck me as being totally true, because my fear was based on fear of something completely intangible which probably didn't even exist, but which kept fuelling the fear anyway – just in case!

I got to the point where I had to stop that process somehow. By realizing how the process was working, I was able to say, 'Hang on a minute, let's take a step back and get a perspective on this.' This was a definite turning point, a barrier which I had to go through and come out the other side of. The alternative was to give up completely and call for help to put an end to my ordeal. I did in fact manage to break through that barrier, and once I reached the other side of it, a great weight seemed to lift off me, just as it had done when I had seen the snake.

After this point, I found that my perspective, which initially had been totally focused on me, my fear and my survival, gradually started to expand outwards. I was able to appreciate more completely the sheer beauty of where I was, the great dome of the sky overhead and the stars like lights of inspiration against the backdrop of the night.

Once my perspective started opening out, I felt very different. I was able to be more centred within myself, more at peace with my surroundings and generally more at one with everything. I felt that I had become a part of my surroundings instead of being apart from them and I started to understand why an Indian who had grown up with a natural sense of harmony with the earth could say, 'You don't need to be afraid of a rattlesnake.' Like attracts like and if you have no fear, then you do not attract fearful things into your life.

It was like moving from a very mind-oriented point of view to a more heart-centred point of being, where your mind doesn't *create* things for you to be afraid of. When you experience that way of being, it takes the pressure off and your mind has no need to work in a negative way as you have let go of the fear that starts the whole process off and which can end up by blocking you completely.

By the time the morning came, I knew that a major change had taken place within me, a whole shift of perspective and understanding that meant that I would never be quite the same again as a result of my whole Vision Quest experience. I had learnt a great deal and knew that I would carry that understanding with me from that point on. I had been enriched by my experience and had realized the value of the Vision Quest tradition as I would not have learnt so much so quickly in any other situation.

Since then, I have found that if I start to feel afraid of something, I can recall the experience of how I felt at the time of my Vision Quest, and I remember what the solution to that was – to let go. Then I am able to let go of my fear. So it helps me to deal with situations even now, and I'm sure that will remain true for a very, very long time.

This second example of flooding obviously required even more courage than the rattlesnake incident. Natasha had quite a long journey to the Vision Quest site so that her fear had become quite considerable even before she started the actual Vision Quest. She was also exposed to fear for hours on end, with no real option of escaping it. Since she did not know where she was in the forest, she could not have run away, even if she had wanted to.

The fact that she was forced to stay and endure her fear, however, resulted in her working out a solution that allowed her to let go of her fear. She realized that she was afraid of something that *might* happen, rather than something that *was happening* at that moment, and with this realization she found that she could relax and even enjoy her time in the forest.

As you can see from Natasha's report, flooding can be a fascinating experience, provided you feel basically stable and your fear problem is manageable.

A man in the US discovered the method of flooding by

accident. He had been suffering from agoraphobia for years and felt practically immobilized by his fear of panic attacks. It had become nearly impossible for him to leave the house, so one day he decided he had had enough. He was so fed up with his agoraphobia and with life in general that he decided to commit suicide. He left his house and took his car out of the garage. Now that he was going to die he didn't care how many panic attacks he was going to have on the way to the beauty spot where he wanted to end his life.

Can you guess what happened? He did not have one single panic attack, arrived safely at the beauty spot, enjoyed the view and returned home, a free man. He had faced his fear and overcome it at the same time.

NUTRITION
Self-help
For all fears

What we eat and how we eat have a greater impact on our well-being than many of us like to believe. Once a particular eating pattern has been established, we lose the awareness of how it affects us. Even when a certain food makes us feel unwell, we tend to overlook the fact after a while, not because we want to, but because we are so used to feeling under par that it no longer strikes us as being unusual or alarming.

All we normally do is to make up for the negative effects in another way. When we overeat, we go on a diet every once in a while – instead of eating less. If eating large portions at meal-times makes us tired, we try and make a bit of time to take a nap – instead of eating lighter meals. When drinking too much coffee makes us nervous, we smoke a cigarette in the (erroneous) belief that this will calm us down – instead of cutting down on caffeine.

Sometimes we are not even aware that certain substances or foods give us problems, and this is one of the main reasons why I am including a section on nutrition in this book. Be on the lookout for any connections between your nutrition and your well-being. Keep a diary if need be so you can monitor if there is a link between what food you consume and how you feel as a consequence; it beats guessing any day!

In this section, I am going to point out some of the most common problem areas that can occur in connection with nutrition and suggest ways in which faulty habits or a deficient diet can be set right.

Eating habits

Many people assume that the process of digestion starts the moment the food has reached your stomach, when in fact, digestion begins in your mouth. It is therefore essential that you should

- *Eat slowly*. Sit down when you eat, don't grab something in passing and wolf it down. *Make* time for eating. Concentrate on what you are eating, don't gobble your food down without thinking. Try not to wash food down with great amounts of fluid because that prevents your stomach acid from working properly and you feel bloated and constipated as a result.
- *Chew properly*. As you cut down the food into smaller bits with your teeth, you enhance the production of enzymes in your mouth which helps break down the food so that your stomach acids can work more efficiently and your body can fully absorb the nutrients, including vitamins and minerals.
- *Drink water*. This is essential for good health and for the kidneys to work properly. Many vitamins and minerals are water-soluble, and their absorption will depend on you drinking enough water. You should drink *at least* one litre of bottled water a day to ensure that your kidneys are flushed through and waste materials can be discharged with your urine.

Eating slowly and chewing properly also makes it easier to eat less, simply because the food stays longer in your mouth and comes in contact with all your tastebuds rather than only brushing past a few of them. This in turn means that you reach a feeling of 'taste-satisfaction' at an earlier stage and feel that you have had enough to eat more quickly.

Being underweight

It is not necessary to be your ideal weight in order to feel fit and healthy, but it makes sense to get as close to it as you can. Rather than being overawed by the various ideal-weight-tables that exist, go for a 'feel-well' weight. (This can sometimes differ considerably from what the tables say you are supposed to weigh!)

You need to be careful, however, if you are extremely slim. When there is no fat on you at all, you are most likely to feed on your nerves when you are in stressful situations. If you have a buffer zone of a few extra pounds on your body, then any physical, mental or emotional exertions will result in a depletion of your fat reserves. This is why people who are going through a traumatic period in their life lose a lot of weight very quickly, even though they may not have reduced their food intake to any large extent.

If you don't have any reserve at all, your nerves are highly sensitized, and things can get to you much more easily. In some people, an extra six or seven pounds can make all the difference. They feel on a much more even keel, and things that used to upset them in the past affect them considerably less.

If you cannot put on any extra weight even though you try, check out with your doctor whether your kidneys function properly. If they don't, it means that your body needs to use up a lot of extra energy to counterbalance the toxins in the body which have not been dealt with because of the malfunctioning kidney(s).

Another reason why you won't put on weight even though you eat normally could be hyperthyroidism (see also p. 33) where the thyroid is working overtime and using up an above average amount of calories, so that these calories have no chance of settling down as fat on your bones.

Other reasons why you stay underweight, even though you don't want to, are a permanently stressful environment, either at work or in your private life. If there is a possibility of improving your circumstances, for example by changing jobs or by sorting out matters at home, then this is of course the best thing to do. However, this is not always possible. Sometimes we are caught up in a situation that is beyond our control. It is still worth your while to start thinking whether you can do anything at least to ameliorate the situation by getting away from it temporarily.

If the reason for your emotional stress lies somewhere in the past, you could go and see a counsellor or therapist to help you sort it out. Often when you have done that, not only does your weight normalize, but your fear has gone as well!

Dealing with hypoglycaemia

I have already mentioned hypoglycaemia in Chapter 1 of the book as one possible factor that exacerbates a fear problem.

First, let me explain to you how hypoglycaemia can come about and how you can check whether you suffer from it.

The body has two regulating mechanisms to maintain an optimum blood sugar level: the upper and the lower.

We maintain a normal blood sugar level by eating carbohydrates which are the energy-giving foods such as starches (bread, potatoes, cereals and rice) and sugars (fruits, honey, refined white and brown sugars). When a large quantity of carbohydrates is eaten, the upper regulating mechanism is activated — there is a surge of insulin and the excess sugar is released into the urine.

If, on the other hand, there is a long interval without food and the blood sugar level drops down to the lower regulating mechanism, the adrenals are mobilized and this in turn releases sugar stored in the liver so that your blood sugar level can return to normal again.

As the adrenals are mobilized, they release adrenalin and cortisol, *and this makes you feel more anxious and can also result in trembling, feelings of unsteadiness and palpitations,* all of which are signs which also precede panic attacks.

If you want to find out whether you suffer from hypoglycaemia, check whether any of the following points apply to you:

— You experience restlessness, anxiety, palpitations or even panic when you wake up in the morning. (In the morning, your blood sugar level is lowest because you have not been able to eat for the time you were asleep.)
— You feel anxious or lightheaded and possibly also irritated

three to four hours after a meal, and those symptoms disappear as soon as you eat something.
- You can feel a clear difference in mood which changes from positive to energetic as you consume sugar to negative and depressed about 30 minutes after ingestion.

Should you have spotted any of these three tell-tale signs, you need to modify your eating habits and be more selective about what you eat. Here are some of the rules.

- *Avoid sugar.* Above all, avoid any foods that obviously contain refined sugars such as chocolate, sweets, ice cream, lemonades and cola drinks. Instead, eat fresh fruit. Avoid fruit juices and dried fruit; both contain sugar in very concentrated form.
- *Avoid simple starches.* These are white bread, pasta and white rice. Substitute the whole grain varieties such as whole grain bread, brown rice, cereals, nuts and seeds.
- *Eat between meals.* Make sure you have a snack at hand between meals, so that your blood sugar level can never fall below the lower limit. Alternatively, you can have five smaller meals a day which you distribute evenly throughout the day, with meals never being more than a maximum of three hours apart.

Masked food allergies

With a masked allergy, detection is difficult because immediately after having eaten it, the food makes you feel better – and this is why people keep eating it. But once you stop eating the food, if only for a day, the true effects come out, and these are usually quite severe. The effects feel very much like withdrawal symptoms – irritability, insomnia, confusion and disorientation, fear, dizziness and depression. All you need to do to switch off these symptoms is to have another helping of the allergenic food and you feel fine, but now you have started the vicious circle again . . .

It can take a lot of willpower to withstand the temptation to go back to the allergenic food, and sometimes it can be useful to get a qualified nutritionist to help and support you.

If you are not aware of any particular cravings, you can still test relatively easily whether you have a food allergy. If, for example, you want to determine whether you are allergic to milk, eliminate milk and all milk products from your diet for two weeks. While you do that, keep a diary of how you feel before, during and after the elimination. After two weeks, drink a few glasses of milk and observe how you feel during the next few hours. If you have a clear, adverse reaction you know that you have found the noxious substance. You can then also test for other substances such as wheat products, eggs, yeast or tomatoes, all of which are quite common allergenics.

Another way of testing for food allergies is to fast for one week, only taking water, and one by one reintroduce foods and observe whether you experience any adverse reactions. This method should only be used under medical supervision and at a time when you can take time off work, especially if you have no experience with fasting. Fasting over a prolonged period of time, that is for longer than a day, can have quite drastic effects on your energy levels and your emotional state, so please make sure you get expert help with fasting.

With any food allergies, I'm afraid the only solution is to stay away from the substance that is giving you the problem, but it is a small price to pay if it helps you remain calm and relaxed and to function normally again.

Vitamins and minerals

Our body is a very complex and finely tuned piece of equipment which relies on a multitude of biochemical processes working smoothly and efficiently. We are normally born with all these processes in pristine condition, but lots of things happen on our way through life to deplete our physical resources. The stresses and strains of everyday living as well as traumatic events in our life take their toll. Refined and processed foods make it harder for our body to do its work, and pollution, additives and preservatives aggravate matters. When you additionally suffer from fear or anxiety related problems, your biochemical processes are knocked off balance even further.

In order to help your system cope better while you have a

fear problem, you should make sure that you supplement your diet with the following vitamins and minerals.

Vitamin B complex

B vitamins help the nervous system function properly. Vitamin B complex is a group of B vitamins which are all water-soluble. This means that it is not possible to overdose on them, but it also means that you have to drink enough water to enable your body to absorb the vitamins.

A deficiency of these vitamins can sometimes produce mental changes which are similar to those of pre-menstrual tension, for example anxiety, irritability, fatigue and emotional instability.
* Take 50–100 mg once a day, *always with food*.

Vitamin C

It is well known that Vitamin C enhances the immune system, protects you from infections and colds and promotes the healing process after illness or injury. Moreover, it helps the adrenal glands function properly. This is important as the adrenals have to work harder when you are under stress or anxious.
*Take 1000 mg twice a day, *always with food*.

Calcium and magnesium

Calcium and magnesium have a soothing effect on the nervous system; they are natural tranquillizers.

If you lack calcium, you feel nervous and on edge very easily. Especially if you are eating a lot of bran you should add calcium to your diet, as bran blocks absorption of calcium.

Always take calcium and magnesium together as they enhance each other's absorption into the body. Take two parts of calcium with one part of magnesium, or combine them on a 1:1 basis. Healthfood shops sell capsules that combine both minerals.

*Take 1000 mg of calcium plus 500–1000 mg of magnesium per day, *always with food*.

Zinc

Zinc has an influence on growth and on resistance to infection. It is also involved in normal hormone production and normal mental function. It has a stabilizing effect on the nervous system and is nowadays prescribed to counterbalance anxiety.

Zinc absorption is blocked by tea, coffee, alcohol and the contraceptive pill.

*Take 200 mg once a day, *always with food*.

Note: Unless you get a zinc preparation that is resistant to gastric juices, you may experience a slight feeling of sickness for a few minutes after ingestion. This is entirely due to the zinc tablets and will go away very quickly.

Substances to avoid

When you suffer from anxiety, there are a few dietary factors which you would do well to banish from your life as they tend to aggravate your problem.

Caffeine

If you drink excessive quantities of tea or coffee, you subject your system to a permanent state of tension and nervous arousal, which is the perfect breeding ground for a panic attack. I am using the term *excessive* here rather than *large* because it will depend on each individual's physical and biological make-up how much caffeine is too much. Some people find that they get the shakes and have to repeatedly go to the toilet after just one cup of coffee; other people need to drink five cups to get the same effect.

The average cup of coffee contains anything from 70 to 150 mg of caffeine; the average cup of tea contains roughly between 50 and 100 mg. Cola beverages are around the 45 to 65 mark per can, and chocolate and cocoa are the lowest with under 25 mg per bar or cup respectively.

Caffeine is addictive and will therefore produce withdrawal symptoms when you try and give it up. Symptoms range from apathy to nervousness, headaches and overeating, but these side effects tend to disappear after a few days, but at the latest after two weeks – provided you stay off the caffeine.

A gentler way of coming off caffeine is to wean yourself off slowly, reducing caffeine intake gradually. You may also find it helpful to substitute tea and coffee by alternative beverages such as herbal teas or dandelion coffee. You will have to get used to the taste of these alternatives because they do not taste like the original, but most people find after a few weeks that they begin to acquire a taste for the substitute.

Please note that drinking decaffeinated tea or coffee is not really an alternative. Even though these tamed down versions contain only a very low level of caffeine, they still contain *some* caffeine, although they are called caffeine-free. Moreover, latest research seems to suggest that the process of decaffeinization involves chemicals which are detrimental to your health.

As with any addictive substance you would be best off giving up caffeine completely. It is easier to stay off coffee if your palate is not led into temptation by the occasional cup.

Nicotine

As discussed earlier, nicotine aggravates a fear problem because it constricts the blood vessels and makes it more difficult for the heart to pump the blood through your system so that the heart has to work harder. This results in a feeling of alertness and arousal which makes any feelings of fear worse. People who claim that smoking helps them relax only obtain this effect because they breathe deeply as they inhale, but it is the deep breath that has the relaxing effect, not the cigarette!

As with giving up caffeine, you may find it difficult to abstain from smoking. Use all the help you can get. Enlist the help of family and friends so that they don't offer you any cigarettes, learn to breathe properly and to relax (see p. 89), or see a hypnotherapist. You will be surprised at how much calmer you feel once you are a non-smoker, and how much extra energy you have once oxygen can circulate freely through your system again.

To help yourself give up more easily, use a trick to make smoking more tedious. Keep your cigarettes at the back of a wardrobe upstairs, and your lighter or matches in the basement or the garden shed. Keep both items as far apart as possible so that you need to get up specially and fetch a cigarette, then go all the way to the lighter before you can actually light up. If it is a lot of hassle to get the next cigarette, it makes it easier to cut down on the number of cigarettes you are smoking.

Once you have stopped, notice how much lighter and freer you feel on a physical level. And anyway, who wants to be a slave to something as silly as some rolled-up dried leaves . . . ?

Salt

If you eat a lot of salt with your food or if you tend to have salty snacks frequently, you are putting extra stress on your heart. Excess salt increases the blood pressure and makes your body retain water, both of which puts extra strain on your heart.

Also, salt depletes your potassium resources, which in turn adversely affects the proper functioning of your nervous system.

Your daily intake of salt should ideally not exceed 1 gram (ca. 1 teaspoon). If you need to add salt, use a salt substitute high in potassium salt, rather than sodium salt.

Summary

The solutions for fear problems as offered in Chapter 3 of this book have been tried and tested and are proven to be successful with a great number of people.

Please feel free to adapt the methods to your own needs; they are not gospel. If you are more comfortable sitting up than lying down for the relaxation, then change your exercise accordingly. If you can only relax if you are standing on you head, never mind that the book tells you to lie down – stand on your head!

There are no strategies and techniques that work for everyone, so it's OK to change them to fit your needs. Be creative. You are a unique individual who does not necessarily fit into the average mould.

The techniques outlined here are effective and very powerful tools, *provided you use them*. I promise you that reading this book may make you feel better, but it will not get rid of your fear unless you get down to the nitty-gritty of doing the exercises every day and keeping at it.

As with everything else in life, you have exactly two choices. You can either leave everything in your life as it is, stay afraid and stop complaining about it, or you can take action and get rid of your fear. It is your decision. I can only show you the way to the water; you have to go and drink yourself. Nobody can do this for you. There is no such thing as a magic wand that will make your fear disappear.

Think about it. What have you got to lose? Only your fear . . .

If you have any problems with any of the techniques, you can contact me personally at the following address:

Vera Peiffer
P.O. Box 2517
London W5 5LN

Further Reading

Relaxation and Meditation

Fontana, D. *The Meditator's Handbook*, Element, Shaftesbury, 1992.
Fontana, D. *The Elements of Meditation*, Element, Shaftesbury, 1991.

Visualization

Gallwey, W.T. *The Inner Game of Tennis*, Random, N.Y., 1974.
Markham, U. *The Elements of Visualisation*, Element, Shaftesbury, 1989.
Richardson, A. *Mental Imagery*, Springer, N.Y., 1969.
Samuels, M. and Samuels, N. *Seeing With the Mind's Eye*, Random, N.Y., 1990.

NLP

Bandler, R. *Using Your Brain For a Change*, Real People Press, Utah, 1985.
Grinder, J. and Bandler, R. *Trance-formations*, Real People Press, Utah, 1981.

Positive Thinking

Peale, N.V. *The Power of Positive Thinking*, Prentice-Hall, N.Y., 1952.
Peiffer, V. *Positive Thinking*, Element, Shaftesbury, 1989.
Peiffer, V. *Strategies of Optimism*, Element, Shaftesbury, 1990.

Logotherapy

Frankl, V.E. *Man's Search for Meaning. An Introduction to Logotherapy*, Simon and Schuster, N.Y.; Hodder and Stoughton, London, 1963.

Alexander Technique

Brennan, R. *The Alexander Technique Workbook*, Element, Shaftesbury, 1992.
Gelb, M. *Body Language*, Aurum Press, London, 1987.

PMS and Nutrition

Dalton, K. *Once A Month*, Fontana, London, 1991.
Stewart, M. *Beat PMT Through Diet*, Vermillion, London, 1992.

Additional Information

Hypnotherapy

International Association of Hypno-Analysts (IAH)
PO Box 180
Bournemouth
Dorset BH3 7YR
Great Britain

The American Association of Professional Hypnotherapy
PO Box 731
McLean
Virginia 22101
USA

NLP

Corporation for Advanced Hypnotherapy
PO Box 70
Southport PR9 9HR
Great Britain

Richard Bandler
2912 Daubenbiss Ave # 20
Soquel
CA 95073
USA

Grinder, DeLozier & Associates
1077 Smith Grade
Bonny Doon
CA 95060
USA

Positive Thinking

The Hypnothink Foundation
PO Box 154
Cheltenham
Glos. GL52 2SL

Alexander Technique

Society for Teachers of the Alexander Technique (STAT)
20 London House
266 Fulham Road
London SW10 9EL

If you would like a list of Alexander teachers who work in Great Britain or abroad, write to the above address and specify which list you want and it will be sent to you.

Counselling

Metanoia
13 North Common Road
London W5 2QB
Great Britain

American Personnel and Guidance Association
Two Skyline Place
Suite 400
5203 Leesburg Pike
Falls Church
Virginia 22041
USA

Kinesiology for Allergies

Jane Thurnell-Read
Health Kinesiologist
12 Castle Road
Penzance
Cornwall TR18 2AX
Great Britain

Index